The Metamorphic
Technique

For more information
contact:
Metamorphic Association
67 Ritherdon Road
London SW17 8QE
01-672-5951

Gaston Saint-Pierre and
Debbie Boater

The Metamorphic
Technique

Principles and Practice

Element Books

*To all those involved in the great mystery
of Transformation*

© Gaston Saint-Pierre and Debbie Boater 1982
First published in Great Britain by
Element Books Limited
The Old Brewery
Tisbury, Wiltshire

Printed in Great Britain by
Robert Hartnoll Limited
Bodmin
Cornwall

Text and cover design by Humphrey Stone
Diagrams by Ray Smith

ISBN 0 906540 20 8

A list of members of the Metamorphic Association is
available from the Publishers. All the members of the
Metamorphic Association are practitioners of the
Metamorphic Technique.

Contents

List of Illustrations

Acknowledgements

The authors would particularly like to thank: Robert St John, without whom none of this might have happened; Jill Archer, for giving us both such strength and support; Kate Prentice, for being there every time Debbie fell; Barbara D'Arcy Thompson, Helen Chittick, Dr Brian Goodwin and Jeffrey Lies for their invaluable advice and criticism; Marigold and Antony Dick, Jenny Young, Guy Gladstone and Osmond Phillips for their help and love; Michael Mann who was the most patient of midwives and made everything possible; and lastly, but by no means least, all the patients, students and colleagues who shared their insights, discoveries, joys and anguishes with us. Thank you.

We would also like to thank the following for permission to reproduce copyright material: John Shane, for his very special "Song of Self Healing"; Harper & Row, New York, for an extract from *Muktananda, Selected Essays* edited by Paul Zweig; Sir George Trevelyan for an extract from Evelyn Nolt's poem as found in his book *Magic Casements*, published by Coventure Ltd; BBC Publications, London, for the extract from J. Bronowski's *Ascent of Man*; Oxford & Cambridge University Press for the extract from the *New English Bible*, Second Edition © 1970; James Rudolph Murley for a quote from his manuscript *The Sanity Book*; Jonathan Daemion, for quotes from his manuscript *Wholistic Phenomenology — Emotion and Consciousness*; Karl König for extracts from *Meditations on the Endocrine Glands*; Newsweek, October 24th, 1977; William Heinemann Ltd, London, for quotes from *The Prophet* by Kahlil Gibran; Robert St John, for extracts from *Metamorphosis*; Wildwood House, London, for an extract from *Bodymind* by Ken Dytchwold; Coventure Ltd, for an extract from *Bioenergetics* by Alexander Lowen; Faber & Faber Ltd, London, for an extract from *Four Quartets* by T. S. Eliot; Delacorte Press/Eleanor Friede, New York, for an extract from *Illusions* by Richard Bach; The Self Realisation Fellowship for an extract from *Scientific Healing Affirmation* by Paramahansa Yogananda, L. A. 1974. Thank you.

Foreword

"The Metamorphic Technique" gives an excellent basis for Metamorphosis, and a means for those who are really interested to reach further into the practice and principles involved. That Metamorphosis is becoming almost universally known is a very exciting fact. The more that is written about it the better.

We have seen in the past how such works can become splintered into various "schools of thought" and this is one of the things that I have tried to avoid in my teachings and writings, and I am delighted to see how the authors have maintained the principle and aims of this work.

The authors have made an extremely well documented approach to all that is concerned in this work and I am confident that this book will open the way for very many students. I look forward to its publication.

November 1981   ROBERT ST JOHN

THE SONG OF SELF-HEALING

Let the healing forces
of the sun, the moon, the stars,
and the planets in their courses
    flow through me,
    flow through me.

And as a river
filled by the rains
returns the waters to the seas,
may I give back,
to all who lack,
the knowledge of the way,
to understand within themselves
the unity of the energy
which dances in all forms,
from the smallest atom
to the greatest galaxy.

And in the splitting of a second,
may I see
the unfolding of infinity
within me
    and so be free,
    and so be free.

Let the healing
power of air,
which all must breathe,
show how we share,
show how we share,
and how
with each and every breath
we balance life and death,
we balance life and death.

Let the healing
power of water
      make me grow
      make me grow
that I may learn
to let go
and live each moment
in the flow.

Let the healing
power of earth
give me new birth,
give me new birth,
that I may see
the equal worth
of all the many
forms of life,
and so, within myself
make an end of strife.

Let the healing
power of fire,
kindle my heart's
true desire,
    draw me higher
    draw me higher.

Let the healing
power of light
make my vision bright
so that in me
all seeming opposites
may unite,
and I may go beyond
both wrong and right
no longer seeing life
in terms of black and white.

Let the healing
power of sound
flow through my voice
to all around,
and tune my ear
to all I hear
so that my mind
may grow clear
and I may be
free from hope and fear.

In centreless silence
let me see
the healing grace
of brilliant luminous
empty space
to be the essence
of my own mind,
and thus may I go beyond
all limited conceptions
of birth and death,
and transcend
false views of time.

By the healing power
summoned in this song
may I,
and all who suffer,
now grow strong,
and may all hearts know
that peace
for which they long.

JOHN SHANE 1978

1 Introduction

. . . . Medicines and food have a definite chemical action upon blood and tissues. So long as one eats food, why should one deny that medicines and other material aids also have an effect on the body? They are useful so long as the material consciousness in man is uppermost. They have their limitations, however, because they are applied from outside. The best methods are those that help the Life Energy to resume its internal healing activities.

PARAMAHANSA YOGANANDA[1]

Over the last 50 years man has experienced an explosion of the boundaries of his mind and of his use of power, as psychology and physics have opened vast new vistas to his understanding of reality. This has created a pool of information, and as more becomes available, our comprehension of the mysteries of the universe expands. Along with this movement, our approach to medicine and therapy has widened and we have gained a greater insight into the workings of the body and the mind as a whole. This has given us the concept of holistic medicine, which recognises that a person must not be treated as a collection of parts but as an integrated living unit, and that within us, we have the ability to heal ourselves.

Among these insights has been the Metamorphic Technique, which embodies this self-healing quality, putting into practice an idea that has recurred throughout the ages. Although it appears simple and obvious, the finite mind has had difficulty in grasping it: Life itself is the great healer.

Life is a factor that pervades, yet is beyond, everything. It is, and acts as, a power in matter and this power we call the life force. Life is creation and from creation comes movement: that movement is change, and it is the life force that sustains this change within the many differing cycles of existence, be it a tree, a planet or a human being. No state can ever be said to be permanent: however slowly there is always movement taking place. The Metamorphic Technique stresses that even beyond this life force, the principle with which practitioners work is, simply, life.

We can compare life to water, which may be in the form of ice, steam, a river, or the sea. There is a continuity of movement throughout these various forms, on many different levels, molecular, atomic and so on. In the river flowing downstream, however, the flow may be hindered by boulders or branches. But always there is the reality of the river beyond the boulders, the potential for change beneath the blockages. So our own movement and ability to change may become blocked but the full force of life is waiting in the wings, as it were, to move us towards a greater state of freedom.

In nature the acorn becomes an oak tree and a caterpillar metamorphoses into a butterfly. We ourselves have within us the potential to do and to become far more than we are at present. We have come into the limitations of matter but we have the ability to experience freedom within those limitations. This ability is an attribute of the life force. Through its workings inner change comes about, not necessarily from any external imposition or intervention. On the instinctual level, all animals, including man, have the power to heal themselves. Wild animals in distress will fast and rest in quiet until they have recovered as no doubt early man did until he lost touch with this instinct. Since that time man's mental faculties have vastly increased, often at the expense of his intuition. And although modern medical science has achieved so much, we still must remain aware that we have our healing power within us.

Life is the power that heals; the use of that power towards self-healing has, through the ages become atrophied. Man now needs a catalyst again to contact and to reawaken this quality. In the Metamorphic Technique, practitioners are catalysts in the same way as the earth is a catalyst. A seed falls to the ground and the earth and the elements simply loosen its physical structure: within the seed there is a power which releases its potential for growth. The practitioner, as the earth, loosens a structure within the patient; like the earth, he is a catalyst, but not for anything in particular. There is a meeting between the earth and the seed which is without needs expressed or imposed from either side: in this work the practitioner and the patient meet, and similarly there are no expectations and no impositions. The purpose of nature is fruitfulness, and the ultimate purpose of life is to fulfil itself always to the highest at whatever level. In man there is that same power which is life, and the inherent potential of his full realisation as a human being. But what is the structure that has first to be loosened?

In many schools of healing and therapy, there is the belief based on the premise that conscious life starts at birth, that our present characteristics are formed in childhood. But, as soon as a cell is created, it has an elementary consciousness. So it can be said that life starts at conception when the first cell is formed.

During the gestation period, the nine months between conception and birth, our physical, mental and emotional structures are established. Our life following birth is rooted in and influenced by this prenatal period, our life before birth. It is this structure of time that has to be loosened.

Many different factors influence us throughout these nine months: the ways of being of our parents, the cultural and environmental world they live in, the evolutionary stage that man has reached, together with non-material, cosmic influences. All these shape and form the patterns of our lives and are primarily established during that time. We are, in essence, the consciousness which is developed during gestation, as a result of all the influences present at conception. The Metamorphic Technique focuses on these nine months. Whereas the earth works with the physical structure of the seeds the practitioner, as a catalyst, loosens a structure which is abstract, a structure of time, that of the gestation period.

This structure has been found to be reflected in the body, particularly on parts of the feet, hands and head; by lightly massaging these areas, that formative period, those nine months, can be brought back into focus and loosened. The practitioner understands that life is doing the work necessary for the patient — the work of change. For this reason, the practice is used not only with the mentally retarded or the physically handicapped, but with all those who are concerned with personal growth. The changes come about through our own power to heal ourselves, to truly create ourselves.

Hence, one of the most important aspects of the

Metamorphic Technique is the attitude of mind of the practitioner. His aim is to work with the life force without imposing his will upon it or directing it in any way. If he desires to help, or to try to channel energy either to or from his patients he is denying their own life the space in which to work. As we cannot smile, or breathe for another person, how can we presume to be able to heal him? The practitioner's attitude we repeat, is to see himself as a catalyst, knowing that it is the patient's own life force which will do what is right.

The work of metamorphosis is expressed through a change in our mode of being. It is a movement from who we are to who we can be. There has to be a letting go of old patterns in order that freedom may be realised, as well as a recognition that symptoms are simply manifestations of life, a part and not the whole. Should the metamorphic practitioner concern himself with the symptoms of his patients, and try to cure them, he would not be working in a holistic way. Symptoms must be irrelevant to him, as the earth takes no account of bumps and scratches on the acorn. As we cannot measure perfection, so we cannot measure imperfection. Each of us is as we are meant to be, at the level of awareness we have reached — at the same time our life force is working towards the fulfilment of our potential as human beings. No one can ever know what that perfection is for another person. The caterpillar is perfect in its stage as a caterpillar; a further stage of perfection will be reached when it becomes a butterfly.

This attitude towards symptoms is an important difference between the Metamorphic Technique and therapies, healing and conventional medicine. It is the life force of the patient, not the practitioner which does the work. The power works within the patient and may contrive various circumstances to bring about a state of integration or wholeness. It has been noticed for instance that a patient may turn to other forms of treatment or medication while the Metamorphic massage is being given at weekly intervals.

The Technique is easily learned. There is no restriction on any person being able to practise it. It can be done by anyone on any other person. For example, it can be practised on a mentally retarded child and that child can do it to others. It is available to everyone, of whatever age, whatever state of health, both as a treatment and as a practice. This book outlines the model we are working with, a practice which is simple because it is just allowing our own life force to work for itself. As catalysts, practitioners do not do the work of change, the life force is in charge. This is obvious because we are life and life itself is the healer.

2 History

Man, tread softly on the Earth
What looks like dust
Is also stuff of which galaxies are made.

EVELYN NOLT[2]

It is proposed nowadays that the origin of the universe is vibration or movement, waves of energy that become radiation, leading to the formation of matter. The different frequencies of these waves create the symphony of the spheres. On earth, for man, movement finds a more specific expression. As J. Bronowski describes: "In a parched African landscape like Omo, man first put his foot to the ground. . . . Two million years ago, the first ancestor of man walked with a foot which is almost indistinguishable from that of modern man. The fact is that when he put his foot to the ground and walked upright, man made a commitment to a new integration of life and therefore of his limbs."[3] By standing upright, man thus began to distinguish himself from all other animals, as he became poised between gravity and levity.

If we pause for a moment and take a look at our feet, they appear physically quite curious: delicate, fragile structures supporting our entire weight, carrying and moving us through our lives; and we can still see patterns of the past reflected in them, such as square feet with short toes that speak of primitive peoples going barefoot, or long thin toes like those of a monkey ready to curl around a branch. Our feet can feel separate, unrelated to the rest of our body and we rarely pay them much attention. Yet we stand, walk, run and move on them every day of our lives, as they are a part of our moving centre, extending from the pelvic area.

From the pelvis down through our thighs, knees, calves and ankles to our feet is reflected our ability to move, both physically and psychologically. Our pelvis is physically the area of birth: through action here a new life is launched into existence. Psychologically we can see it as the area in which we are able to give birth to ourselves, to let go of old patterns and processes, to move into new areas. This movement of creation flows down into our feet which are the most outward expression of ourselves in the world; when we walk our feet go forward first. Movement is essential: "In the beginning was the Word. . . ." and the word is sound wave, vibration, movement. Without movement there is no life, so the feet, as an extension of the moving centre in the body, are an expression of this primary function of the universe. In the Tao Te Ching we read: "The journey of a thousand leagues starts from where your feet stand."

Our feet portray how we are in the world, how balanced we are in ourselves. The rigid heavy foot often corresponds to rigidity in the person, a strict or unbending nature; weak insubstantial feet can indicate how the person has an inner weakness, timidity, or is possibly in a state of collapse. Feet that point in opposite directions, the right going one way while the left goes another, can show a person who is confused about his direction in life or who is never sure which way he should move. "Standing on your own two feet", "putting one foot in front of the other", "having both feet on the ground", are all phrases used to express our relationship with reality, with the world, just as "knowing where you stand" is an affirmation of our position in life.

Our feet form our base, our foundation, on which we are balanced, through which we are supported and from which we reach upwards. We talk of being "rooted", "grounded", of someone who is very "earthy" implying someone who is in touch with reality. We talk of being "uprooted" when we feel lost, alienated or separated from our past, our family or home. The psychological connection between mother and earth is expressed when we talk of a baby "rooting" for the nipple.

As we think about our feet more deeply, their importance becomes clearer. They are our link with the earth, our bridge between the higher realms and the worldly, physical realms of our being. For all the spiritual or intellectual flights we may take, there has to be a point where our higher understanding of life is earthed, is brought into actuality. Our feet symbolize this earthing; the way we stand or walk, the way we balance ourselves, indicates how we are in the world, the path we are treading, the direction we are moving in; and as such the feet represent the whole of our being.

We can see this link at work in some of the major religious expressions. For instance, at Bodhgaya in India, where the Buddha gained enlightenment, we find the "Jewel Shrine of the Walk" with giant footsteps carved in stone and the "miraculous lotus blossoms that sprang up where he walked". It can also be seen within the tradition of kissing the feet of a master — a way of the disciple humbling himself as well as a way of touching and showing reverence to the understanding manifested in the master. We find that Jesus, while washing the feet of his disciples, in reply to Peter, says: "You do not understand now what I am doing, but one day you will." Peter said "I will not let you wash my feet." "If I do not wash you," Jesus replied, "you are not in fellowship with me." "Then, Lord," said Simon Peter, "not my feet only; wash my hands and head as well."[4] This indicates, perhaps, that unless we are washed clean of the patterns of the past, then we cannot enter into the realm of freedom. Swami Muktananda, a contemporary Indian teacher, says: "The Guru's feet are like the foundation on which a building stands, but they should not be confused with certain physical limbs. When Jnanshwar says 'I worshipped the Guru's feet' he is referring to something more than his physical body . . . Awareness of one's identity with the Guru is true worship of the Guru's feet."[5] Thus the way in which our feet link us with the earth also creates this deeper symbolism, that of the manifestation of our higher nature in matter.

We have seen the importance of the feet from various viewpoints, but how was this importance originally recognised? Five thousand years ago, the Chinese observed that there were parts of the body which communicate with the outside world, the nature of that communication differing according to the part used: the head, through the senses and the brain, is the channel of communication with the heavens; the hands, through touch and creative expression, are our channel of communication with each other; the nipples, through nurturing and sensuality; the anus, not only through defecation, but also through sensuality, especially in young children; the genitals, through bearing new life, as well as through sensuality; and the feet, through our movement in the world, being our channel of communication with the earth. It was when we first stood upon our feet that the polarity of heaven and earth came into being, symbolised by the yin and yang forces of energy in Chinese philosophy. From that first observation, the Chinese went on to discover that these areas mirror the body, that each area on its own is a microcosm reflecting the whole body within it, thus communicating the body through it, to the outside world.

Medical care at that time was related directly to the understanding of man as a whole being, not just a collection of parts. The body and mind were seen as one, so if an illness occurred, it was recognised as an illness of the whole being. It was believed that the connecting link throughout is energy, known in China as Ch'i or, as we have already termed it, the life force. Illness was seen as an imbalance or blockage of this energy, that for some reason had got "stuck", so medical care was aimed at balancing or freeing the blocks in order that the energy could flow again and heal the illness. It was found that every part of the body is on one of various pathways or meridians of energy: an inner organ could be reached by working on points along the pathway related to it. Methods used were acupuncture, where needles are inserted to stimulate the energy, shiatsu, where pressure is used instead of needles, and massage.

Every organ was seen to have reflex points, points that correspond through energy to the organ, in other parts of the body, some of the most sensitive of which are found in the feet, the hands and the head. This approach to medicine was researched and developed into Zone Therapy at the beginning of this century by an American doctor, William Fitzgerald. He divided the body into ten zones from the head down to the fingers and toes. The energy flowing through these zones goes through the body to the reflex points in the hands and feet. His work was later extended by Eunice D. Ingram into Reflexology, a form of compression massage concentrating almost entirely on the feet, that differs only slightly from the original Chinese approach.

Wherever there is an illness, we can find a corresponding area in the foot where there may be pain or waste materials in the form of tiny acid crystals forming on the energy pathway. Reflexology works by massaging the feet, breaking down these crystals, smoothing out the pain and restoring the energy to a state of balance. As the feet are being treated, the patient may momentarily feel a sharp pain when the energy is freed, but will then experience a release throughout the whole body. The energy that flows within us that connects our being into a living whole, is the energy that maintains our health. When it is freely flowing then we are well, balanced, in harmony with our environment physically, mentally and emotionally. Illness, in any form, is an imbalance, a congestion of this energy.

From the charts *(See Figs 1 and 2)* we can see how all the various parts of the body fit onto the feet. They are like a mirror with the left and right feet reflecting the left and right sides of the body. The toes reflect the head, brain, eyes, nose, mouth and sinuses. The soles reflect the internal organs, the bony structure of the foot reflecting the framework of the body. The heels reflect the pelvic area including the organs of reproduction and elimination. The spine is reflected in the bony ridge on the inner side of both feet from the first joint of the big toe down to the heel bone. The upper corners of the big toe nails reflect the pineal gland and the lower corners the pituitary gland. A line across the top of the foot from under the inner ankle bone to under the outer ankle bone indicates the reflex area of the pelvic girdle. It is interesting to note that many different charts have been made, showing the various reflex points at slightly different places on the feet. Yet the treatments seem to work no matter which chart is used. It can only be concluded that much of the healing lies in the release; that it is the stimulation of energy rather than of a specific point which encourages the healing power to be active.

Reflexology has been found to have remarkable effects on illnesses ranging from arthritis, migraine, constipation, ulcers and kidney infections to angina and bronchitis. In some parts of the world, foot massage is a fully accredited medical treatment and is often used as an accurate form of diagnosis, foretelling disturbances in the body long before they become physically apparent. In Indonesia, for example, it is a traditional practice for a family to massage each other's feet regularly to prevent illness, correcting imbalances before they become serious.

Reflexology demonstrates how the feet reflect the body and that the results are not achieved through activity in the nervous or circulatory systems as there are no direct physical links between the inner organs

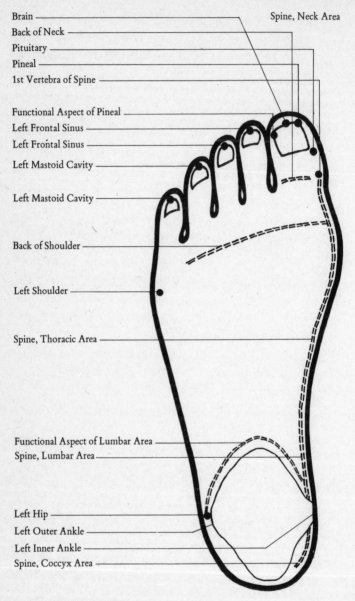

Brain —

Back of Neck —

Pituitary —

Pineal —

1st Vertebra of Spine —

Functional Aspect of Pineal —

Left Frontal Sinus —

Left Frontal Sinus —

Left Mastoid Cavity —

Left Mastoid Cavity —

Back of Shoulder —

Left Shoulder —

Spine, Thoracic Area —

Functional Aspect of Lumbar Area —

Spine, Lumbar Area —

Left Hip —

Left Outer Ankle —

Left Inner Ankle —

Spine, Coccyx Area —

Spine, Neck Area

1   *Reflexology chart of the upper surface of the feet*
     as formulated by Robert St. John.

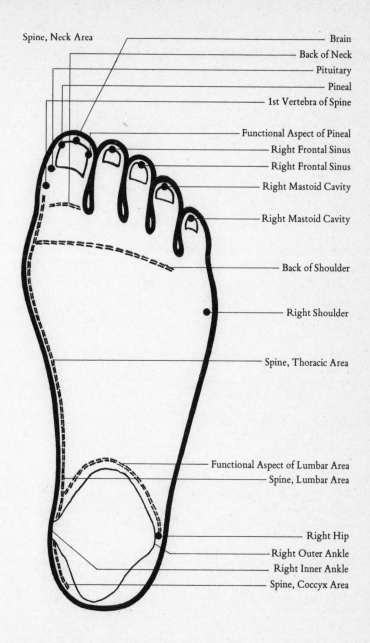

Spine, Neck Area

Brain
Back of Neck
Pituitary
Pineal
1st Vertebra of Spine

Functional Aspect of Pineal
Right Frontal Sinus
Right Frontal Sinus
Right Mastoid Cavity

Right Mastoid Cavity

Back of Shoulder

Right Shoulder

Spine, Thoracic Area

Functional Aspect of Lumbar Area
Spine, Lumbar Area

Right Hip
Right Outer Ankle
Right Inner Ankle
Spine, Coccyx Area

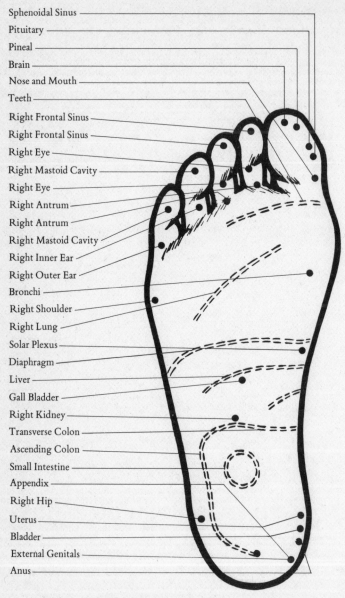

Sphenoidal Sinus

Pituitary

Pineal

Brain

Nose and Mouth

Teeth

Right Frontal Sinus

Right Frontal Sinus

Right Eye

Right Mastoid Cavity

Right Eye

Right Antrum

Right Antrum

Right Mastoid Cavity

Right Inner Ear

Right Outer Ear

Bronchi

Right Shoulder

Right Lung

Solar Plexus

Diaphragm

Liver

Gall Bladder

Right Kidney

Transverse Colon

Ascending Colon

Small Intestine

Appendix

Right Hip

Uterus

Bladder

External Genitals

Anus

2   *Reflexology chart of the lower surface of the feet
as formulated by Robert St. John.*

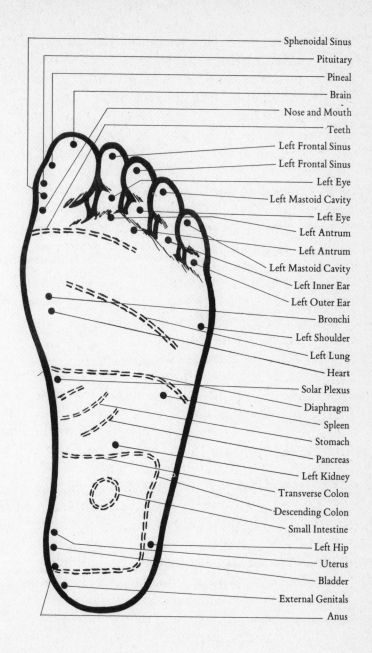

Sphenoidal Sinus
Pituitary
Pineal
Brain
Nose and Mouth
Teeth
Left Frontal Sinus
Left Frontal Sinus
Left Eye
Left Mastoid Cavity
Left Eye
Left Antrum
Left Antrum
Left Mastoid Cavity
Left Inner Ear
Left Outer Ear
Bronchi
Left Shoulder
Left Lung
Heart
Solar Plexus
Diaphragm
Spleen
Stomach
Pancreas
Left Kidney
Transverse Colon
Descending Colon
Small Intestine
Left Hip
Uterus
Bladder
External Genitals
Anus

and the feet. It thus suggests that it is through the energy system within us that we are able to heal ourselves. Physicists explain the same thing in another way: that in the amazing intricacy of the human body, every cell is a hologram containing the knowledge of every other cell and therefore of the whole being.

Out of Reflexology came a development of great importance, initiated by Robert St John. A naturopath of long standing, he had become dissatisfied with general nature cure practice because he had come to recognise that we create our own stresses, the cause of the illnesses, and that these stresses fall into two distinct classes: those that pull away from life and those that push too forcefully into life. This is exemplified in the extreme by the autistic and the Down's syndrome persons. The current methods of treatment did nothing to help these proclivities.

This dissatisfaction with his work led him to explore Reflexology. He found that the various systems used were all so different that it seemed, at that time, that one or more were wrong and that he would do best to find out things for himself. Nature being the best teacher, he created his own charts of the reflex points on the feet, as he found them. From here, his intuition led him to realise that many of the ailments found in the body as reflected in the feet, could also be related to a corresponding blockage in the spinal reflexes; the massage was just as effective when he worked only on the spinal reflex area and not the whole foot.

As the spine, the main bony support for the body, contains the central nervous system and as there is no separation between body and mind, Robert St John's attention was drawn to observing the psychological effects of the treatment. Whilst working on the heel area, he noticed a corresponding association within the patient with what he came to call the mother principle. If there were blocks or imbalances in that area, which reflects the base of the spine, the sexual organs and the place of birth, so there were seen to be difficulties with either the relationship between the patient and his mother, or with the mother principle within the patient himself: the ability to express caring, nurturing and receptive qualities. Later observations by practitioners brought about the realisation that there may also be difficulties in being earthed, being in touch with reality, being well grounded. Having found the mother principle around the heel area, there came the logical question, where was the father principle to be found? When working on the area around the first joint of the big toe, which corresponds to the upper neck where the nerves come out of the brain into the spinal cord, if there were blocks he found corresponding psychological difficulties in the patient with the father principle, the external father or authority figure. Later observations showed that there may also be difficulties with the patient's expression of his own inner authority or fathering qualities, the right to be himself, and even the right to be at all.

To recognise these psychological states, Robert St John had had to raise his vantage point by superimposing a psychological map upon the physical reflex map. He then raised his vantage point still further. Through insight he saw that between the father principle at the toe and the mother principle at the heel, lay a reflection of another map, a time map, of the nine months we spend in the womb. The spinal reflex points are thus recognised as a support for a structure of time. It is at conception that the father could be said to be the most active, as it is only here that he fully participates in the creation of the new life. Obviously the mother also participates at conception, but through giving birth finds the fulfilment of that participation. Between these two events, we have the gestation period. Therefore, while we work on this area, we are actually working on the time structure during which all our characteristics were primarily established.

It was in the 1960's that Robert St John made this discovery, one that had been hinted at by the traditional acupuncturists in China. He first called it Prenatal Therapy, since its concern is with one's prenatal or gestation period. It later came to be called the Metamorphic Technique. The principle of self-healing and the possibility of a cure being permanent occurred to him when he started practising his own version of Reflexology (reflex therapy then).

We focus on this prenatal time not as something past, but as an integral part of our present. In this sense, time is like a river flowing from a lake into the sea, where moisture is taken up into the atmosphere to return again to earth and repeat the cycle. The events of the past are still in some form of existence. In "Birth Without Violence", Dr Frederick Leboyer suggests that the spine holds every memory of our prenatal time within it, explaining how it is through our spine that we are in constant contact with the walls of the womb and with every movement that takes place within our mother. So it is on the spinal reflexes that we find the prenatal pattern.

A new map has been discovered, showing an earlier

picture of the area than was hitherto recognised. First, we have the map of Reflexology, showing the physical body reflected on the feet. Then we find there is a psychological map beneath the physical. Beneath the psychological we find a map of the gestation period, but if we look beyond that map too, then we find life itself.

It is here that a clear distinction between Reflexology and the Metamorphic Technique can be seen. Reflexology works to bring about changes within the body, primarily on the physical level. The Metamorphic Technique works in another way, on a time level, and it allows the life force to bring about the change within the patient. The Reflexologist may work specifically on areas corresponding to illnesses in the patient so as to help alleviate those illnesses, whereas the Metamorphic practitioner takes no notice of symptoms or illnesses but works always on the prenatal pattern, as the area representing the time when our weaknesses and strengths were first established. With this practice, changes may manifest themselves on the mental, emotional and behavioural levels, as well as on the physical level. The practitioner focuses on a time structure, pointing to the life force flowing through it. We do not look at the territory of symptoms and illnesses but at life itself. If we hold onto the map we will not be able to see the terrain around us; we have ultimately to let go of all the maps we have used and consider them only as references, in order to see the land, to see the life.

Why is it that we don't work directly on the spine but go instead to the spinal reflex points on the feet? By working on the spine, we would be effecting immediate changes and imposing a direction to those changes, through our very manipulation. The primary issue is that blockages in the gestation period are the causes of the ailments. Incidental to that issue is the relationship of the gestation period to the spine, that the stresses of that period should manifest in the spine and from there to the body. So the layout of the Reflexology charts becomes irrelevant as we work in the abstract, as it were, on a time structure. We use the reflex system, and more specifically the spinal reflex area on the feet as a support for that period of time; that enables us to work from an attitude of detachment.

Since the gestation period belongs to the past, it follows that the work of the Metamorphic Technique is concerned with that time. But time is not something linear; the events of the past are still with us. By loosening the time structure, the life force of the patient can alter the characteristics laid down or formed in the past (which are still effective) and release them, thereby creating a greater inner freedom. In this way the patient's ability to heal himself is truly at work.

3 The Prenatal Pattern

Time is the continuum through which
We experience the changes
In our psychological spaces.

JAMES RUDOLPH MURLEY[6]

One of the many wonders of birth is the extraordinary realisation that here is a new person, fully conscious with its own thoughts and feelings, complete and totally separate. We can understand and accept that physically this being was formed and grew within the womb of the mother, yet so many times the questions are asked — how did it get here? where did it come from? — questions asking not about the physical being but about the inner being, the energy, the consciousness within the body. Watching the birth of a baby, we cannot help but see the individual life as intangible, indefinable, obviously something that is not physical. The mother has been aware of this for some time as the child moved inside her, yet awareness that it has its own consciousness is not so fully apparent until birth. So it is at the marvel of birth that we are confronted with the universal questions of life: where do we come from and why are we here? For the moment, let us consider the questions: when do intelligence and life enter the new being in the womb? Are they somehow present in the sperm and the egg? Do they enter at birth? And if not, then when?

We cannot say specifically when or how intelligence or life enter the body or where they come from, as much of what we understand can only be based on our intuition and assumption. There are many different theories and beliefs as to how we became the individuals that we are. These theories range from us being somehow "made" by God, to being a result of deeds enacted in previous lives, to being a part of a "universal plan", to simply being a product of our parents joining together. There are as many theories as there are questions. We find descriptions of consciousness entering at conception, at 3 months, at 6 months and at birth. Despite the differences however, what is clear is that there is consciousness present before we take our first breath. This can be seen whenever a baby is born and is still attached to the placenta but has not yet started breathing for itself. The baby may well have its eyes open and be exploring with fingers and toes, is very definitely conscious but is not yet breathing. It is a miraculous sight as it somehow confirms the intuitive knowledge that the unborn foetus is conscious.

To attempt an understanding of who and what we are we have to assume a starting point, so let us take conception, as this is the time when we are first formed in matter. Whether consciousness is fully present then or not we do not know; what is important is that in that moment we are manifested on earth in a physical form. All living beings have certain basic characteristics which they share, such as the capacity for healing and regeneration, for making a whole out of a part; or the ability to adapt to changes in the environment, such as tanning in the sun. The process of embryogenesis, the creation of the individual being which follows conception, is one which reveals in a most beautiful manner the making of a whole out of a part, which then links it directly with the healing process itself.

The ovum and the sperm are parts of the mother and the father. At conception they unite to give a single cell which contains the genetic inheritance from both parents. This cell, the zygote, then undergoes a series of transformations whereby a new whole organism is created from the parts of the parents, and this new individual will have particular properties such as eye colour, shape of nose, blood type, etc., which are largely determined by the genes inherited from the parents through the ovum and the sperm. Each individual thus has two "strands" to his or her inheritance: the universal generative properties which are responsible for such processes as embryogenesis and healing, which transform parts into wholes; and particular characteristics which are "carried" by the genes and express themselves within the living transformational process. This inheritance links the individual to all other living beings, so that one may say that all organisms share the same potential for the manifestation of living "intelligence". This intelligence may be understood as the laws of organisation which govern the living state. In embryogenesis, this is made manifest in the orderly transformations which the developing embryo undergoes, first in the cell divisions of the zygote, then in the progressive emergence of spatial order as the cells organize themselves into patterns and produce structures such as head, eyes, and limbs, all in their proper places and functioning together as an integrated whole.

From that first cell the human embryo goes through many different stages of development. In conventional embryology we find a description of the embryo, which at first seems to be a mere streak, but then extends both longitudinally and laterally. There is a school of thought that correlates this growth to the development of consciousness, calling the longitudinal growth "cephalo-caudal development" and the lateral growth "proximo-distal development".

Cephalo-caudal development is the movement from the brain down to the base of the spine, a downward expansion. Jonathan Daemion says of this movement: "The physical development of the embryo, then, suggests a mass of life energy concentrated in the head, which begins to push down, vivifying and forming the lower areas of the body progressively".[7] Proximo-distal development is an outward expansion, a movement from the spine as the centre of the body outwards through the limbs. "If consciousness depends to any large extent upon the development of the physical body as the vessel of consciousness, then the consciousness of the embryo proceeds from an enclosed 'centre' outwards to the more exposed extremities".[8]

A third development is expressed in the theory of recapitulation, whereby the embryo, at various stages, resembles the embryo of other life forms, from the fish, bird, to the mammal. This could be said to show that, in terms of consciousness, not only does the evolution of mankind appear to be present through the genes, but also the whole evolutionary process of life, that through evolution man reflects all other life forms.

Looking at the manifold ways in which consciousness evolves during the growth of the embryo we can understand ourselves more fully as we are now. The ways described above also relate to another way which is called the prenatal pattern in the Metamorphic Technique. Here, remembering that the cephalo-caudal movement of consciousness in the embryo goes downward from the head to the base of the spine, the reflex point for conception is therefore at the top of the spine and the one for birth at the base. The proximo-distal movement, from the spine outwards to the extremities, can be looked at from another viewpoint, that of the baby in the womb to the baby out in the world. This can also be seen as our energy being expressed from a centre outwardly through thinking, doing and moving, through our head, hands and feet.

Let us now look more closely at the prenatal pattern that Robert St John discovered to be of such importance, with the help of the chart that he devised *(See Fig 3)*.

Pre-conception

Here the consciousness of the life to be is, in the abstract, moving towards the moment of conception. This is a stage out of time, space and matter, where it is assumed that the influences that will be precipitated at conception, are being attracted towards that new life.

Conception

This is a focal point in time, a coming together of all the factors that are going to form the new life. We have already seen how the first cell formed by the union of the sperm and ovum contains the full genetic pattern for that new life, every cell thereafter containing this original pattern; therefore, at this point, the "blueprint" of the future being is present, to be developed throughout the following nine months. In terms of consciousness, it is a precipitation into matter of all the influences and characteristics that form our being. It is

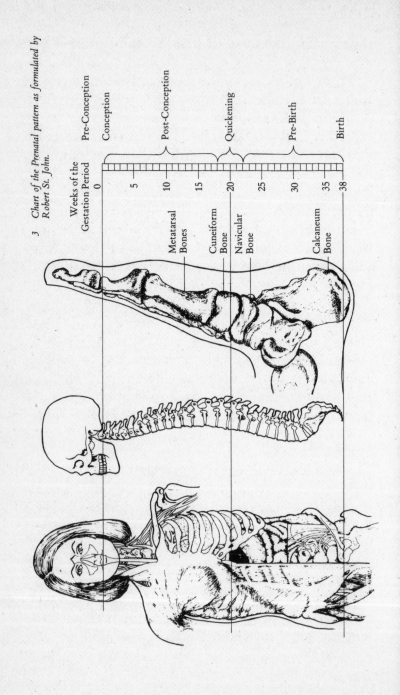

3 *Chart of the Prenatal pattern as formulated by Robert St. John.*

Pre-Conception

Conception

Post-Conception

Quickening

Pre-Birth

Birth

Weeks of the
Gestation Period

0

5

10

15

20

25

30

35

38

Metatarsal
Bones

Cuneiform
Bone

Navicular
Bone

Calcaneum
Bone

the starting point for the individual person we are now.

This moment in time corresponds to a point on the foot at the first joint of the big toe. This is the reflex point for the atlas bone, the top vertebra of the spine.

Post-conception

This is the first 4½ months, from the moment of conception to the 18/22nd week, a time of intense physical growth, a formative, inward developing period when the embryo is establishing itself in matter. In terms of consciousness, there has to be a commitment to life which seems to take place around the 6th week as this is the time when our lungs are being formed, our means for an independent existence. If this commitment is not made, then there may be a spontaneous abortion around the 6-10th week of pregnancy. The embryo, after this early stage, becomes involved with establishing itself as an individual. So the formative period proper, a maturation process on the individual level, starts at the 6th week and lasts until the 18/22nd week.

The word individual comes from the Latin "individuus", i.e. without division. In this sense, the *true* individual experiences no division, is totally at one with everything else. So here, the new life, whilst forming itself as a separate being, simultaneously knows no difference between itself and its environment. This can be seen in a paradoxical way, as an unawareness of personal individuality and as an awareness of true individuality.

Post-conception corresponds to the area between the first joint of the big toe to the centre of the arch between the internal cuneiform and navicular bones.

This point on the foot reflects the area from the top of the spine down to approximately the 8–10th thoracic vertebra.

Quickening

This is when the mother first feels a definite movement of the baby within her womb. It is a turning point for the foetus, as now with its body established, it will begin to move outwards, to explore its environment. In terms of consciousness, this period of time between 18/22 weeks, shows a movement of awareness from self to other than self, from an introverted state to an extroverted one, from the inner development to an outward expansion. It is therefore a time of complete change, an opening of awareness.

Quickening corresponds to the point on the foot between the cuneiform and navicular bones, which reflect the 8–10th thoracic vertebra.

Pre-birth

This period is from the 18/22nd week until birth. The body is formed, but it is not ready for birth, for the outside world. The foetus needs this time for preparation. It will be getting ready to move from the womb, an enclosed, intimate place, to an open and social one in the world outside. It is establishing here the qualities of interaction and communication. The individual as an entity is formed and is becoming aware of itself as separate, perceiving the external environment as something within which it moves, which it both fights against and flows with; it is also aware of its ability to act. Hence this is a time of preparation for action.

Pre-birth corresponds to the area from the centre of

the foot to the heel, which reflects the spine from the 8-10th thoracic vertebra to the coccyx.

Birth

This is obviously a time of great change and a time for action or non-action. The foetus normally motivates the time of its own birth when it is ready for this change. At birth the child and the mother both face the end of their unique relationship as they become two separate beings. Depending on the circumstances, this will give rise to either fear, isolation, panic and withdrawal, or to joy, confidence, unity and expansion. In terms of consciousness, the action that takes place will determine whether there is a sense of freedom or restriction in life, at those times when we are confronted with change.

Birth corresponds to the point on the heel where the Achilles tendon meets the bone, which reflects the base of the spine *(See Fig 4)*.

It is perhaps not surprising that we find re-enactments of this unfoldment of consciousness in the womb occurring throughout our lives. For example, mental disturbances, tensions and anxieties will often be eased or released by a greater awareness of the body, by moving down into the lower part of the body, thus bringing the awareness out of the head as in the cephalo-caudal movement. Similarly, physical disorientation, external chaos or an inability to cope with the world is often relieved by coming into one's "centre", as in the proximo-distal movement, centring into the heart or solar plexus and moving outwards from there, clarifying our sense of direction and our capability.

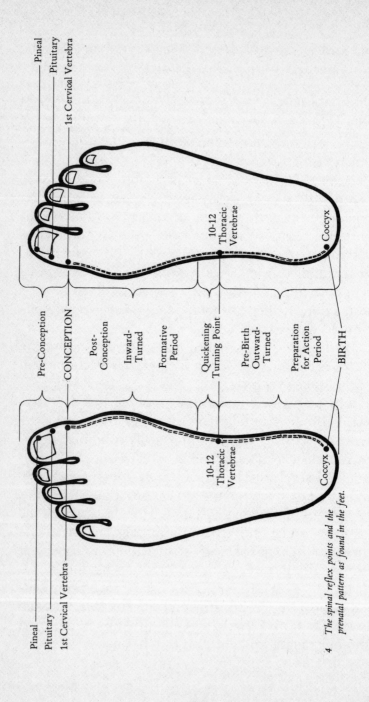

Pineal
Pituitary
1st Cervical Vertebra

Pre-Conception

CONCEPTION

Post-
Conception

Inward-
Turned

Formative
Period

Quickening
Turning Point

10-12
Thoracic Vertebrae

Pre-Birth
Outward-
Turned

Preparation
for Action
Period

BIRTH

Coccyx

Pineal
Pituitary
1st Cervical Vertebra

10-12
Thoracic Vertebrae

Coccyx

4   *The spinal reflex points and the*
     prenatal pattern as found in the feet.

Looking at the prenatal pattern we can also see a re-enactment of this pattern in our lives, for example, in the emergence of a new idea. The formative and developmental stage is followed by the expansion of that idea to see how it can be applied. Then comes the time for action, communication of that idea, criticism, applause or comment by the world at large. The process of birth, in whatever form, be it mental, emotional or physical, is often a painful, dark, confusing time, one of constriction and expansion happening alternately, one of not being sure where you are going but knowing that you have to get there. This pattern also corresponds to that of the human life. Equating conception to the point of birth, babyhood corresponds to post-conception, where there are no boundaries between ourselves and others; the more sociable and extrovert stage of adolescence to quickening when our bodies are fully formed but we are not yet mature; and adulthood to pre-birth. In every birth there is a death: the death of the mother and child as one into the birth of two. In every death there is a birth: the birth of limitlessness out of individuality.

We have already seen how we reflect the whole evolutionary process in ourselves, so we can extend our understanding of the gestation period one stage further by establishing another parallel, whereby our conception can be equated to the beginning of time and our birth to the moment of union of the sperm and ovum. In this way we extend far beyond our own gestation period to the concept of timelessness being contained in our feet. Thus there are three patterns to be found: one, from the beginning of time to the moment of our conception; two, from conception to birth as we have already seen in detail; and three, from our birth to the present point in our life. Therefore we span timelessness and time.

Having traced the development of consciousness through the gestation period, we can now look more closely at our original question, where does this consciousness come from? Surprisingly, this relates to recent thoughts on the endocrine system, in particular to the pineal and pituitary glands, both situated in the brain. The endocrine system as a whole is a collection of tiny glands that excrete minute amounts of hormones, regulating all functions in the body from thinking to reproduction. The system is autonomous, operating "on its own" and could thus be likened to man's instinct, responding immediately to stimuli and maintaining a balance within the bodymind. A good example of this is the release of adrenalin due to the stimulus of fear.

The pineal is a mysterious gland that seems to have no direct function, yet in severe cases of mental disorder, the calcium crystals normally present are often missing. Dr Karl König says of this gland: "This organ remains in a veiled and mysterious form within our body . . . it lives in us like a seed-bud of a plant, the rest of which has withered away. Like the ovary of a plant . . . impregnated by the eternal ideas and giving to man the possibility of forming his own conceptions. It is an organ of thought, by means of which we learn to 'know' and thus to change eternal ideas into earthly conceptions. Here lies the reason for Descartes' statement that the pineal gland is the seat of the human soul. The pineal gland keeps the gate open between our soul and the realm of the spirit".[9]

This suggests that the pineal gland is the entry point of consciousness, the highest point of knowledge within us, yet almost dormant in modern man. It is interesting to note that above this gland is found the fontanelle, which remains open in us until well after birth. Below the pineal comes the pituitary, known as the "master gland" of the endocrine system as it directly influences all the other glands. Here it would appear that the higher knowledge of the pineal is being channelled onto earth through the pituitary: "If the pineal gland points to the land of the spirit, the pituitary points to the earth. The human soul awakens to earthly consciousness by means of this small organ".[10] Confirming this in the scientific world were the co-winners of the 1977 Nobel prize, Drs Roger Guillemin and Andrew Schally, for their work on hormones, in particular the pituitary gland: "Their research may explain how the mind affects the physical and mental well-being through hormones . . . It's a link between body and soul".[11]

In terms of consciousness then, we find the pineal gland as the seat of absolute knowledge and the pituitary gland as the seat of the higher mind.

We have seen how the genes from our parents literally "build" us, but still we have not answered our question of where consciousness comes from. Obviously we are now back in the realm of assumption. Before conception, in the abstract, there seems to be a movement of energy and consciousness towards a focal point. From there the energy will be transformed so that it can be precipitated into matter at conception. In terms of consciousness, that focal point becomes, after conception, the pineal gland and the stage of transformation becomes the pituitary gland.

To simplify this, let us take the analogy of the creation of a house. An architect thinks of building a house, then sits down to draw the plans. The builders, with their materials, will then build it following the instructions of the blueprint. For a human being, the parents are obviously the builders. It is easy to think that the genes are the plan, yet can they be said to contain the personality, the individuality? If not, then one has to assume that at conception there is a coming together of the builders and the materials, with the architect. The original thought of the architect to build a house is analogous to the pineal gland, and the drawing of the plans to the pituitary gland. In the preconception stage, intelligence was therefore designing the blueprint of the new life, gathering, as it were, the colours that would influence the purity of that life, as it moved towards the first cell formed by the parents' union.

To expand the analogy of building a house, the Chinese remind us that we do not live in the bricks but in the holes in-between them, the rooms. Our parents may have provided the building bricks that built us, but the space within us is where our higher consciousness may be found.

4 Principle of Correspondences

That which seems most feeble and bewildered
In you is the strongest and most determined.
Is it not your breath that has erected and hardened
The structure of your bones?

KAHLIL GIBRAN[12]

Apart from the prenatal pattern there are other patterns or maps in the body, all of which help us to see how we function as an integrated whole. The importance of the concept of "bodymind", that there is no separation between the body and the mind, cannot be stressed enough. We tend to think that we "have" a body, that we give our body exercise, food, rest, pleasure or medicine when "it" is ill. We see our body as something we carry around with us; we like parts of it but dislike other parts; we worry when something in it goes wrong, but what we usually fail to see is that it is not a part going wrong, it is the whole of ourself. When we feel depressed, our body feels heavy and lifeless; when we feel happy, we feel light and vibrant. Our mind and body work as one.

Everything in the universe, which includes everything that makes up our self, *is* energy. That energy may take different forms but whatever the form, whether it be a physical condition, a mental conflict, an emotional joy or a spiritual realisation, it is energy. When there is disharmony within us we may get a bad cough, feel angry, get a pain in our back or become disorientated and confused. If we bring together the psychological and the physical, then we can understand that there is no difference, whatever the mode of expression may be: the underlying imbalance is simply energy needing an outlet. We can, from here, begin to learn how to "read" the body, to see what the imbalance is that is taking place on all levels. To help us there are certain signposts, one of which is the principle of correspondences.

This approach, developed by Robert St John, had its inspiration in the Doctrine of Correspondences as formulated by Emanuel Swedenborg, a Swedish religious teacher who lived in the 18th century. It proposed that every natural object is congruent to, and symbolises, some spiritual fact or principle. A close relationship can thus be inferred between spiritual qualities and material forms, the former being archetypes of the latter. This idea can then be applied when we consider the three primary ways in which life manifests itself in man, as energy, as mind and as emotion. These correspond to the three main cellular structures of the human body: hard tissue, soft tissue and fluids.

Hard tissue

The hard tissue within us is mainly found in the skeleton, the structure and core of our physical being. It can be correlated to the rocks and minerals of the earth, providing a solid, inner foundation. Bones form our basis, a framework upon which we are built. They can be seen as the physical manifestation of energy that came in at conception. As Robert St John explains: our bones "portray the primary pattern of that with which we started life at conception" containing "the inherited traits, the karmic patterns and all the other factors which are imposed upon or drawn into the new life. The spine is the centre of this structure and expresses the prenatal pattern which is the focal point of this work. The rest of the skeleton is the extension of this principle into the three forms of . . . thinking, doing and going, . . . as expressed through the head, shoulders and pelvis."[13] Portrayed in the hard tissue is our desire to incarnate, to actually come into matter. For life to manifest, it must have a form which is our skeleton.

Scientists have found that, the more compressed the matter, the faster the atomic particles within that matter move, and so the more atomic energy there is. As such, diamonds contain the greatest quantity of atomic energy as they are the most compressed form of matter. Within man we can see a correspondence between the bony structure and the energy aspect of our being, as the bones have the most compacted atomic structure in the body and therefore, the most condensed form of energy.

It is interesting to note here that a similar concept is used in the Alexander Technique which aims to create harmony and balance by loosening the skeleton and teaching the correct use of it, so releasing and balancing the energy. It is also the bones that are the main structure worked with in Pulsing, a form of massage where the body is rhythmically rocked throughout the treatment. Here the purpose is to help release emotions and traumas locked in the skeleton.

We have seen that there is a correspondence between the bony structure and the energy aspect of our being. If we now displace our vantage point, energy becomes power, and what is the ultimate power? "Thus said the Lord God unto these bones; behold, I will cause breath to enter you, and ye shall live."[14] The Latin word for breath is "spiritus", i.e. the animating or vital energy in man, that which gives life to the physical organism, in contrast to its purely material elements. The highest power then, is this "breath" of life or spirit.

The bony structure is the pattern we start with. The soft tissue structure is what we make of this pattern.

Soft tissue

The soft tissue within us is our skin, flesh, organs, nerves and muscles, and can be correlated to earth. The flesh and skin provide a covering for the bones; the muscles, tendons and ligaments give them movement, strength and flexibility; the internal organs, directed by the autonomous nervous system, maintain the bodily functions.

Our soft tissue corresponds to our mental aspect and expresses the continual movement of change within ourselves. The muscles provide the means for the hard tissue structure to move, and in the same way our mental aspect enables us to move and change in accordance with our insights and understandings.

Our soft tissue portrays our deeper characteristics, traumas and experiences. As Ken Dytchwold says in his book, *Bodymind*: "I have come to see that . . . psychological choices and personal attitudes and images not only affect the functioning of the human organism but also strongly influence the way it is shaped and structured."[15] Those who walk upright, with strong legs and a straight back can be said to be facing the world with confidence, whilst those with a bent back and lowered shoulders may be carrying a psychological burden of some kind. Tensions get locked in our muscles — rigid tendons indicating rigid tendencies — slowly building up to cause the energy to get blocked or held. The memory of past events gets built into our tissue, causing actual changes in the physical form. Alexander Lowen, in *Bioenergetics*, writes: "A person is the sum total of his life experiences each of which is registered in his personality and structured in his body. Just as a woodsman can read the life history of a tree from a cross-section showing its annual growth rings, so it is possible . . . to read a person's life history from his body."[16]

When we talk of our mental aspect, consciousness is implied. To be conscious we have to be conscious of something, there has to be an object or an idea on which to focus our attention. The Buddha likened consciousness to a flame passing from one log to another; the flame cannot exist without the logs, as consciousness cannot exist without an object. And yet one feels that there is something at work, something that exists beyond the reality of the object. This is intelligence. In terms of Swedenborg's Doctrine, the Sufi quotation expresses this: "Intelligence faced with an object becomes consciousness."

The soft tissue gives us movement, and it is the fluids that give direction to that movement.

Fluids

The fluids within us — the blood, water and lymph — permeate and flow throughout our entire organism, affecting health and balance. They correlate to the oceans and rivers, flowing throughout the planet. When we are aroused there is an immediate change in the fluids: blood suffusing lips, nipples and genitals, or an outpouring of sweat. Approximately 90% of the body is fluid, mainly water, which acts as a great internal sea flowing up and down, with waves and currents affecting the direction of the flow.

The fluids correspond to our emotional aspect. The word emotion is derived from the Latin: *e-movere* — to move out; our emotions express the direction of the movement of change within us and they give drive and purpose to that movement. Physicists tell us that the galaxy is expanding from the centre outwards, that there is an outward direction in the movement of the universe, as in the proximo–distal development. We could say that one of the reasons of our being on earth is to expand in consciousness; it is our emotional aspect that gives direction to the expansion.

The highest form of emotion is ecstasy. The word is not used here with religious connotations, but as an expression of man's ability to go beyond his rational limitations.

The hard tissue is enabled to move by the action of the soft tissue and that movement has order because of an implicit sense of direction. Our energy aspect underlies our mental and emotional aspects just as our bones are beneath the flesh and fluids. As we grow in awareness, our being is "stepped up" and we begin to function more on the higher levels of spirit, intelligence and ecstasy.

Hard Tissues	Structure	Energy Aspect	Power	Spirit
Soft Tissues	Movement	Mental Aspect	Consciousness	Intelligence
Fluids	Direction	Emotional Aspect	Feeling	Ecstasy

5   *Chart of the Principle of Correspondences.*

This principle of correspondences *(See Fig 5)* provides us with a map to read what is happening in our being. As an illustration of this we have the words of Robert St John: "Muscular troubles indicate inactivity of the mobility of the mind. Heart troubles indicate an aspect of the mind which is at variance with the capacity to permeate the structure with the life giving nourishment, with the penetration of the 'Life' into every cell. It is an emotional factor. Liver troubles indicate an inhibition of the principles of action in the capacity to get on with the maintenance of life. Bladder troubles indicate a conflict with the capacity to free oneself of the emotional patterns of the past. The hardening of the arteries indicates a rigid attitude towards the free flowing of feelings."[17] We can extend this approach still further as there is another signpost pointing towards an understanding of our being, that is the function of the various parts of the body.

The understanding that the Chinese had about the six areas of communication, namely the head, hands, nipples, anus, genitals and feet, gives us an insight into how the bodymind relates to the world. The reason why the head, hands and feet are massaged in the Metamorphic Technique is because these three external communication areas correspond to three primary actions: thinking, doing and moving or going *(See Fig 6)*. In any well balanced function in life, we would use all three almost simultaneously: the initial inspiration, the execution and the movement of the action.

The moving or going centre extends from the pelvic area to the legs and feet. Activity here expresses our ability to move physically. Our feet represent that moving quality as well as extending out into the world

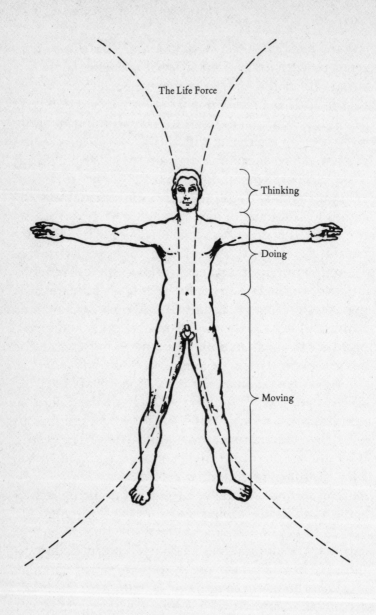

The Life Force

Thinking

Doing

Moving

6   *Chart of the thinking, doing and moving centres.*

first and furthest when we walk. The massage on our feet focuses on the movement of change within us, it may affect the way we are moving in the world and how we feel about the direction we are taking. It gets things going. The moving centre also corresponds to the pre-birth and birth stages of the prenatal pattern which are connected with our social and outward going aspects.

Situated at the upper part of the body we find the doing centre, extending out from the spine, to the shoulders, the arms and the hands. It is through this centre that we express our executive, creative and giving qualities, what we are doing with our life and how we handle it. Through having our hands massaged, our ability to do things within the movement of change and our feelings about what we are doing in the world are released. The doing centre also corresponds to the post-conception stage, to the personal and inward turned aspects of ourselves.

The head is considered the centre of planning. Every action that we take is initiated from the brain to the body via the central or autonomous nervous system. We think out our action before we perform it, we plan and we act. Through the brain we project our thoughts out into the world and we receive ideas and thoughts from others. The head is a major centre of communication, through which we perceive the world by way of the senses: seeing, hearing, smelling and tasting. The way in which we see ourselves in the world and think of ourselves in relation to it is also connected to this planning centre. Having our head massaged helps release our ability to think, to govern our life and to have initiative within the movement of change triggered off by having our feet massaged. The thinking centre corresponds to pre-conception and conception, to the receiving and understanding of energy and knowledge.

These three centres of activity correspond to the three main ways in which we express ourselves. For example, our feelings emanate from the core of our being and we express them upwards and out through the head by the use of our eyes and mouth, our voice and words and in kissing; outwardly in our arms and hands through holding, stroking, touching and comforting; and downwards through our pelvis by the act of loving, thus giving, sharing and communicating.

As we now draw a larger map of the bodymind we begin to see how a physical malfunction can be related to the mental and emotional levels, and vice versa. We bring together three things: the function — thinking, doing, moving, and the form of the part affected — hard tissue, soft tissue, fluids, together with the prenatal pattern, e.g. the correspondence between the chest and the post-conception period. Let us take some examples to show how this works, bearing in mind that here we are looking at the manifestations of life, the parts and not the whole. Our main concern is always with the power of life over and beyond the maps or symptoms.

Urinary infections, cystitis, etc: this condition is located in the pelvis, and the pelvis corresponds to the moving centre. As the fluids portray the emotional aspect, so the urine relates in particular to negative emotions, which "poison" internally. The pelvic area also corresponds to the pre-birth period when the ability to be a social being is laid down. Therefore the emotions expressed will be directly concerned with other persons. So it could be said that urinary infections are showing an emotional conflict with the movement taking place in life, or, specifically, difficulties with people, maybe anger or frustration. It is as if there is an emotional holding back so that the energy finds expression in a physical way. Research has shown that more cases of cystitis occur in women when there are relationship difficulties than at any other time.

Sore throat, cough: a sore throat indicates irritation of the soft tissue in an area connected with the doing centre, what we are doing with our life. The throat is also the energy pathway between the head and the rest of the body and so it can show more than any other area a bodymind split, where the head becomes psychologically divided from the body. In the prenatal pattern, the throat and chest correspond to the early part of the post-conception period and to inwardly turned energy. So what is being suggested here is a mental irritation, a frustration or conflict within ourselves, regarding what we are doing, or going to do, with our life. There can be a mental resistance to expressing ourselves in words and a separation from the feelings in our body.

A cough indicates mental irritation bringing up unwanted fluid, phlegm, or unwanted, unacknowledged emotions. We want to "get something off our chest", feelings we are holding back and not fully acknowledging, especially to ourselves. There is also a mental resistance to expressing our feelings.

This way of looking at the bodymind is important to our understanding of the difficulties we encounter, and to what they are saying to us. The bodymind will try to show in many ways that there is something wrong, that there is a blocking of energy, before it has to resort to pain. It will use symptoms, whether a cold, a headache, constipation or depression, to indicate that there is something on another level which is not being looked at, and so is being blocked.

All this is reflected in the feet, and in reading the feet, we have no need to look at the rest of the body. There cannot be life without movement; the feet are reflecting the movement taking place on every level within us, so their language can be the only guide we need. But we all have our own way of expressing our bodymind, so it is never possible to say precisely what is happening. When we notice a particular condition of the feet, we can be sure that there is an activation of energy, but its expression may be varied. To explain this further let us look at the three aspects, energy, mental and emotional as we find them in the feet.

Dryness: this will show either that the emotional aspect is fairly well balanced, or the emotions may be withdrawn, held inwardly; a lot of moisture may indicate an emotional conflict or a release, an outpouring taking place. With puffy or swollen feet the fluid is being held back, straining against the skin. This can be seen as excess emotion being held at bay, or the emotional aspect meeting with mental resistance.

Callosities: here the skin is hardened, indicating a mental activation of some sort. It is mostly found at the heel which is the area of the mother, the earth principle where the qualities of loving, nurturing or nourishing are present. Here hard skin may represent conflict with our own actual mother, or with those caring qualities within us, as well as the inability to fully incarnate, to be grounded and at one with the world. A callous skin is defined as hard or horny tissue; when the adjective is applied to people it means unfeeling, unsympathetic, crassly indifferent to others' pain. So hardened skin on the heel may show a mental resistance to the mother principle or to matter.

The sides of the big toe are the reflex points corresponding to the father, God principle, and if the callosity occurs there, it indicates a mental resistance to authority, power and responsibility. There may be conflict with these qualities because of resistance to an external source of power or because of the inability to assert one's own inner authority, one's sense of responsibility. This area is also reflecting our point of contact with the heavens, the polar opposite to the earth.

Corns: here the conflict goes even deeper than with callosities as corns have roots penetrating below the skin into the flesh. As there is also pain involved, it indicates an inverted movement of energy, a refusal of the mind to actually look at the underlying conflict. Small corns or a thin layer of callosities that have not been there long show that the disharmony is relatively recent. But a long-term corn or thick chunk of hard skin shows that the problem is of long standing on the mental level.

Peeling skin: this condition often comes and goes, can move around the foot and suddenly vanish, only to reappear later. It is again an activation of energy on the mental level but this time it is a clarification, as when the peeling stops, fresh skin is left beneath. Mental layers of resistance are being removed, are breaking down as we come to terms with various parts of ourselves.

Blisters: here an external irritation causes the skin to erupt with fluid, and this shows mental and emotional disturbances coming to the surface at a point of weakness. It does not necessarily express an inner movement of change but may be simply an indication of weakness, stimulated by an outside agent such as rubbing shoes.

Chilblains: these are caused by a lack of blood into the toes and can be seen as an emotional withdrawal from reality, perhaps because of fear, uncertainty or a lack of clear direction, so that the emotional energy is not actually in touch with the part of you that is moving in the world. This gives rise to mental conflict, which is indicated by the chilblain itself and the sensitive skin. Chilblains appear physically when the weather is cold, and this also shows emotional coldness, a lack of involvement causing mental pain. The toes correspond to the senses, the head and preconception, so chilblains may express a resistance to the full use of the senses or a refusal to really look at what is happening in one's immediate life.

Ingrown toe nails: these appear at the upper corner of the big toenail, which is the reflex point for the pineal gland. The condition shows a mental resistance to the reception of higher energy and to movement or change on that level. Without this energy the nail lacks support and will curl into the flesh.

Bunions: this bone formation indicates a deep conflict on the energy level, corresponding to the post-conception period. The seed of that conflict was planted around the 4th to the 6th week of embryonic development when the lungs were being formed, and the foetus had to make the commitment to being alive. Our lungs enable us to breathe, to sustain ourselves. There may be an uncertainty, a hesitation before the commitment is entered into and that initial reluctance is a weakness which we re-enact time and again throughout our lives — an inability to be fully present in ourselves. There can be a feeling of worthlessness and inadequacy giving rise to frustration and resentment. Bunions often start when people allow themselves to be robbed in some way of their own initiative, their sense of individuality, or when they surrender responsibility for their own life to another person as can happen in a very intense relationship.

Fallen arches, high arches: this part of the foot relates to the area around the solar plexus, which in the prenatal pattern is the reflex area of the quickening stage, and therefore the passage between the way we are in ourselves and the way we are in the world. Fallen arches express a collapse on the energy level, a feeling of weakness and hopelessness in our relationship with the world and our ability to move in it. They show a tendency to skim over the surface of the earth, like a water boatman on a river, because of fear of getting involved. High arches show a withdrawal, a holding back, an inability to give easily and a reluctance to be involved. They show a preference for the air rather than the ground.

Toes curled up or back and hammer toes: these all indicate a withdrawal of the senses and a lack of desire to be here, affecting consciousness on the everyday level. There is an unwillingness to be present in the world and to move forward in it.

The feet show us what is taking place within ourselves. As an example, a journalist and teacher, when first receiving the Metamorphic massage, had a lump of flesh covering the quickening point at the mid-arch of his foot. This man had many difficulties in meeting and communicating with people, although that was his profession. During a series of treatments he experienced, over a few nights, a sharp pain in that area on his foot, which he scratched in his sleep. The lump disappeared soon afterwards and the quality of his relationships improved considerably.

Look at the chart of the prenatal pattern and you will see where on the feet the various stages of development occur and what they mean. Follow it through to what is happening in yourself. It is all there, recorded in the hard and soft tissue and the fluids. Everything that we are right now — our state of health, our feelings, thoughts, aspirations, difficulties — all of that in this very moment, can be found. Watch out! The person next to you may be able to read your feet like an open book!

5 Influences

*And is it not a dream which none of you remember
having dreamt, that builded your city and
fashioned all there is in it?
. . . And if you could hear the whispering of
the dream, you would hear no other sound.*

KAHLIL GIBRAN[18]

Underlying the question, where do we come from, is another, possibly more important one, which is, what is our purpose for being here? It is an ageless question, asked by man and answered by the prophets and sages time and again. The answers take many forms but speak of the same thing: that man's purpose is to discover his true nature, to gain enlightenment, to realise his full potential, to reach a state of oneness. The paths to such a state are many and varied, the journey can be long and often seemingly impossible, yet it is the ultimate journey man can make, driven on, as it were, by a divine homesickness.

If this is man's true purpose, why does it seem so difficult to achieve? Within all of us flows the pure life stream, taking us through life from one day to the next. Yet as rocks are thrown into the stream causing whirlpools, waterfalls or diversions, so difficulties impede the flow of our energy which becomes blocked. If it were free, our path would be a simple one; it is the eddies and dams, the pebbles and boulders that create the difficulties that blind us to our freedom. Yet the boulders in our way are actually our stepping stones, each an opportunity to grow and reach out beyond our present state, to discover the deeper purpose.

To take an example, let us watch a group of children planning the building of an obstacle course on a lawn. For this they bring materials which they arrange along its perimeter. As they start playing and go through the course, they encounter a wobbly plank that they have to walk along. They fall many times before finally finding their balance. Once they are proficient at the course, they forget about it and go away. From this, we can draw the following parallel with the prenatal pattern: the planning of the game and the gathering of the materials represents the pre-conception stage, as the incoming life attracts to itself the influences that will "colour its purity". The building of the course corresponds to the whole gestation period during which these influences are established. The playing of the children on the course represents life from birth onwards. To take this parallel further, we shall assume that from the vantage point of the Absolute, the purpose of our being here on earth is known before conception. In order to fulfil this purpose at both the cosmic and the individual levels, certain characteristics are gathered together when we incarnate. But this absolute knowledge is then left behind so that it may be rediscovered at an earthly level. The characteristics serve as the means for that discovery. Because we are on earth, and not in the Absolute, we have to learn within the confines of time. In the same way the child, walking along the wobbly plank, falling and starting over again, through repetition discovers how to manage it, and beyond that, the purpose of the exercise, which is balance.

We attract the reality we need. Everything that we encounter in our lives, whatever it may be, is the means for us to expand as individuals. The incidences we attract do not arrive on our doorstep arbitrarily but are what we need, for whatever reason at that time, although we may not recognise this at a conscious level. All the incidences we encounter could be said to stem from "holds in time". To understand this concept, imagine someone coming into our room and shouting at us. We get tense and whenever we meet that person again we remember the event and feel the tension. The event has become frozen in time. The same occurs also if someone says something beautiful to us. The compliment stays with us and gets held in time; it may be recalled and allowed to influence our feelings about the person who said it. Energy becomes diverted, keeping these occurrences present in ourselves.

And so the foundation of our present reality is established through holds in time. All the aids and opportunities, hindrances and difficulties in our life, are with us as a result of the initial patterns formed by the influences precipitated at conception. It is our attitude of mind that will turn this programming into either opportunities or obstacles. A person may develop a very severe illness at middle age, the underlying weakness being present at conception but not becoming apparent until all those years later. The person's attitude may turn this seeming disaster into an opportunity for inner growth or alternatively it may be regarded as a catastrophe. If the former, it will be an aid to recovery; if the latter the trouble may continue for a long time.

To understand this better, let us look at all the factors present at conception, factors that will affect what we are to become. They divide into two categories: material influences and non-material influences *(See Fig 7)*.

Material influences

Material influences are those that we inherit from our parents through the genes. The genetic structure determines some of our characteristics, the fact that we are human, that we belong to a particular race and parentage and are born at a certain time.

Agreeing to incarnate means that we take on all the attributes and qualities of a human, as opposed to those belonging to the animal, vegetable or mineral kingdoms.

The race that we are born into has its own culture and traditions. It has its physical and mental characteristics, emotional and behavioural tendencies that influence each member. These qualities also affect us on a more specific level as we consider the ancestral inheritance that comes through our parents, i.e. the colour of our eyes, congenital illnesses, family and class conditioning. The physical, mental and emotional state of our parents at the time of conception, and throughout the following nine months, will also have a direct bearing upon us. The time of our birth has its importance — to be born in 1982 is very different from having been born in 1902.

The genetic structure of our parents produces our physical being, with the genes rightly called the building bricks of matter. If we look at our brick house, we see not only the walls and foundations but also the

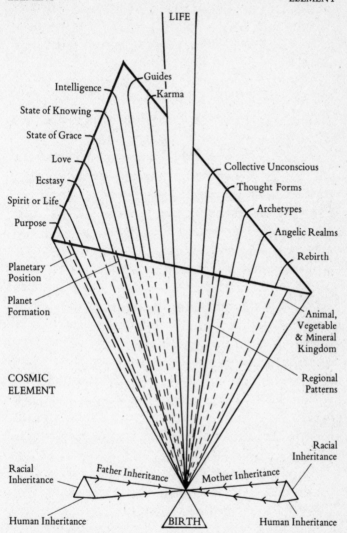

UNIVERSAL
ELEMENT

HUMAN
ELEMENT

LIFE

Guides

Intelligence

Karma

State of Knowing

State of Grace

Love

Collective Unconscious

Ecstasy

Thought Forms

Spirit or Life

Archetypes

Purpose

Angelic Realms

Rebirth

Planetary
Position

Planet
Formation

Animal,
Vegetable
& Mineral
Kingdom

COSMIC
ELEMENT

Regional
Patterns

Racial
Inheritance

Racial
Inheritance

Father Inheritance

Mother Inheritance

Human Inheritance

Human Inheritance

BIRTH

7   *Material and non material influences.*

spaces enclosed by the walls. This space, the rooms and their dimensions, will also influence the inhabitant. So, we have non-material influences which are just as present, but harder to define, than the material ones.

Non-material influences

These are of three types: the human element, the cosmic element and the universal element.

The influences we find in the human element are those either recognised or created by man or those at work in the mind without our necessarily being aware of them. They include, among others, the archetypes and the collective unconscious which have been studied by man especially during the 20th century; thought forms, created by man; the angelic realms and the guides, be they masters, saints or prophets, believed to oversee the balanced progression of man's evolution; karma and rebirth which are an expression of a universal law.

The archetypes are original forms or qualities expressed in man through his psyche, shaping the way his conscious mind operates. The collective unconscious is the memory shared by all mankind of our evolutionary process, and affects man's present understanding of his reality.

Thought forms are creations of man's mind about or around an event or happening; through the power of thought, these creations may take on a life of their own and can affect people even unconnected to these events.

The angelic realms and the guides have been recognised as energy forms working from a dimension higher than the one man is functioning on. As such, they form the hierarchy of the government of the world, inspiring and helping man in the unfoldment of his evolutionary process.

Karma is an expression of the law of cause and effect, that there cannot be a thought, action or event without there being an effect. As everything in the universe is energy at varying degrees of intensity, it follows that even a thought is a wave of energy, like a ripple on a pond. With karma, there is the concept of energy flowing from one life to another, the concept of rebirth or reincarnation. What we do in one life is said to affect the quality and events of the next life, just as what we do in one day affects the conduct of the day that follows.

The influences we find in the cosmic element are also recognised by man, but recognised as outside forces not necessarily under his control. They include planetary position, planet formation, regional patterns and the animal, vegetable and mineral kingdoms.

There is the popular belief that the position of the planets at the time of our birth exercises a definite influence upon us and that astrology is the study of the map of the heavens then. However those who study astrology believe that the position of the planets at the moment of birth provides us with a map of the psyche which, when used sensitively, can help us realise our potentials. It has been observed that many aspects of our character corresponding to the zodiacal signs in which the planets are placed at the moment of birth resemble those of others born under a similar configuration. Similarly the patterns of the individual and the collective psyche are reflected in the cycle of the zodiac, e.g. the passage from the Piscean age to the Aquarian age.

Planet formation includes the phases of transformation the planet has gone through with the movement of the poles and continents. These phases, and the influence of the sun and the moon, will be felt by us as we live on the planet, and as our body is made of the same elements from which the planet is made: earth, water, fire and air.

Regional patterns relate to specific influences exerted by each area of the earth. As a living body, the earth fulfils various functions, so needing and using different energies. The energy in Central Africa will fashion a type of awareness differing from that found on the shores of Britain.

The interaction of the animal, vegetable and mineral kingdoms produces a dynamic equilibrium in the environment. Within them is a consciousness with which man can communicate, e.g. nature spirits and *devas*. But it is possible for him to over-identify with them. The work of these kingdoms is beneficial to man, for example forests producing oxygen.

The influences we find in the universal element are those states that man can know, beyond his normal experience of reality. We usually view reality as it is expressed in matter, time and space. Beyond that, yet always with us, we find purpose; intelligence, the highest form of mental energy and the state of "knowing"; love, the state of grace and ecstasy, the purest emotion; and spirit or life, the expression of absolute energy.

All these influences are like the notes of music, but the music itself, the essence, the sound, is life.

How and why these influences affect us is not always easy to understand; we have to step outside our usual framework of reference and raise our vantage point from our normal conception of time and space. Let us first look at the way these influences materialise.

An analogy with electricity may help. The life force is like the power within a generator. For that electrical power to be made available in matter as an electric fire, it has to be stepped down through a transformer. The electric fire can only function because of the resistance it has against the greater electrical flow. In the same way, before conception, there is life, but for it to manifest in and as matter, the vibrational rate of its force has to be stepped down. This stepping down then attracts the influences that are the resistance to the greater flow of life.

Our characteristics precipitate into matter at conception as potential, and this potential becomes actualised as the embryo evolves. At the physical level, for example, there is in the first cell the potential for the formation of the eyes and their colour, the ability to see and a particular type of vision. The potential in that first cell later becomes active as programmed. Something similar occurs on the more abstract level with the non-material influences. If, having built our house, we discover a crack appearing in the wall, we may find that it is due to a structural fault. It does not help to simply cover the crack over, the fault will still be there and other cracks will appear later. The original fault may have been very small — like a nail put in the wrong place — but it will create chaos on every level. There is no point looking at the damage the nail has done. We have instead to look at the time when the nail was put in, asking ourselves why that particular nail was used in that way.

We can see this further by imagining that we arrive at conception with a bag of mixed seeds which we plant throughout the following nine months. A winter cabbage is not planted at the same time as a spring lettuce. The actual time the energy is stepped down will determine the nature of the later characteristics or difficulties. The seeds then grow into plants according to their season, some of them taking years to mature.

Let us recall the analogy of the river and the boulders thrown into it. The chart over the page *(See Fig 8)* depicts two streams coming to a meeting point, representing the parents meeting at conception, bringing with them their human, racial and individual inheritances. Their coming together allows the non-material influences to be anchored in matter, in the first cell. The single stream goes on to become a river, entering the sea at birth. The boulders in the stream and river are the "holds in time", determining our positive and negative qualities. By looking at the chart, we can see on which level and where these manifest, bearing in mind that this is simply an intuitive attempt to position some of the influences. It is a guideline, a suggestion, not to be seen as fully comprehensive or final, and open to approach from many different angles, to being changed or added to. We can look at the qualities on the chart as tendencies rather than fully developed states of being.

For the purposes of the picture, the areas covered by the stream from conception to birth correspond directly to the headings below. Pre-conception, however, is not related to the two streams above it.

Pre-conception can only be seen in the abstract.

The chart depicts the correspondence of the prenatal pattern to the influences on the physical, mental, emotional and behavioural levels. It is presenting some of the qualities that affect us. They are expressed in one or more of the above ways through which we are active. Again, we must remember that we are considering a part and not the whole.

If there is a purpose for us being here on earth, both on the cosmic and the individual levels, then one way or another, we are working that purpose out with whatever characteristics we have attracted to us. We must recognise that we usually allow ourselves to be at the mercy of the influences, but the choice to transform them is ours. We may, for example, be working under considerable stress and suffer a heart attack, but if we had learnt to realise the condition we were in, and relax, the heart attack might not have been necessary. When we practise the Metamorphic Technique, we can work through the influences by focusing on the life force beyond them. So we realise that we are able to choose if we are to be affected by them or not.

Lessons can take a lifetime to learn, but it is important to remember that influences are merely manifestations of life. Beyond every one of them there is life and the potential for movement and change. Learning is in time. By pointing to the moment in time when the influences were first established, they and the learning process can be brought together, so the purpose is realised and the influences rendered unnecessary. With the Metamorphic Technique, the learning is done "out of time". This however may not be recognised, nor happen on a conscious level.

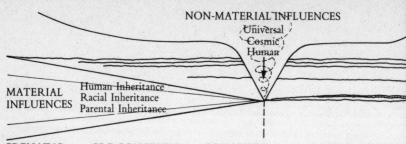

NON-MATERIAL INFLUENCES

Universal
Cosmic
Human

MATERIAL INFLUENCES
Human Inheritance
Racial Inheritance
Parental Inheritance

PRENATAL PATTERN	PRE-CONCEPTION	CONCEPTION	POST-CONCEPTIO 1-22 weeks
PHYSICAL	Head, Pineal & Pituitary glands, Blindness, Deafness, Migraine, Brain damage, Epilepsy, Colds, Influenza, Teeth, Sinus, Meningitis, Multiple sclerosis	Neck, 1st thoracic vertebra, Thyroid, Tonsils, Speech defects, Dumbness, Glands.	Chest, 1-10th thoraci vertebrae, Kyphosis, Lungs, T.B., Bronchitis, Coughs, Heart diseases, Angina, Asthma, Breast cancer, Pleurisy, Frozen shoulder, Pneumonia.
MENTAL	Knowledge, Intelligence, Power, Spirit, Purpose, Wisdom, Truth, Light, Retardedness, Autism, Down's syndrome, Intellectual disorientation, Powerlessness.	Understanding, Energy, Faith, Order, Consciousness, Unknown fears, Abnormal madness and genius, Dyslexia, Inner chaos, Schizophrenia, Ignorance, Fragmentization.	Certainty, Belief, Serenity, Absorption, Commitment, Psychosis, Inward turned energy becoming negative, Self-obsession, Lack of commitment, Implosiveness Depression, Introversio
EMOTIONAL	Abandonment, Peace, Ecstasy, Fervour, Grace, Glory, Sacrifice, Coldness, Loss, Isolation, Total chaos.	Intuition, Surrender, Ardour, Solidity, Sadness, Reserve, Confusion, Fear, Disorientation, Withdrawal, Drivelessness.	Passion for life, Radiance, Tenderness Heartache, Worthlessness, Frustration, Resentment, Dislike (self, Fear of rejection
BEHAVIOURAL	Mystic, Meditation, Ability to transform, Impassivity, Recluse, Ascetism, Splendor, Androgeny, Leadership, Murderer, Violence, Despot, Mystic, Recluse.	Morality, Integration, Confidence, Scrupulousness, Sense of direction, Sense of unity, Purity. Eccentricity, Disconnection from body, Lack of direction, Lack of confidence, Isolation, Lack of scruples, Amorality.	Austerity, Sufficiency, Spontaneity, Ability to feel, Self-honesty, Eternal adolescent, Full of ideas but unable to express them, Self-punishing, Masochism.

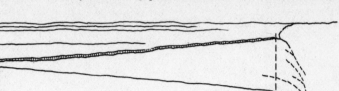

VICKENING 22 weeks	PRE-BIRTH 18-38 weeks	BIRTH
ar plexus, 8-10th racic vertebrae, mach, Ulcers, ut, Hepatitis, ndice, Liver, Gall lder, Gall stones, een, Pancreas, betes.	Lower abdomen, 10th thoracic vertebra to coccyx, Intestinal difficulties, Diverticulitis, Constipation, Cystitis, Bladder, Kidneys, Prostate gland, Infertility, Menopause, Appendix, Reproduction.	Genitals, Coccyx, Impotence, Frigidity, Orgasm, All V.D. infections, Haemorrhoids.
areness, Hope, ceptance, Concern, rvous breakdown, vness, Fear of known, Fear of lity, Fantasy, himsicality.	Morality, Strength, Patience, Understanding, Capability, Growth, Immorality, Neurosis, Extroversion, Paranoia, Other worldliness, Materialism, Sloth.	Courage, Potency, Security, Fearlessness, Confidence, Depression, Defensiveness, Lack of idea actualisation.
rmth, Sensitivity, ness, Calmness, xiety, prehension, bility to express ptions, Guilt, patience.	Cordiality, Compassion, Devotion, Generosity, Charity, Sympathy, Hysteria, Despondency, Anger at others, Coldness, Panic, Lust, Envy, Rejection of others, Greed.	Joy, Love, Expansion, Anger, Terror, Fear, Grief.
ance, Certainty, husiasm, nmunication, giveness, atleness, eathercock drome (going nd and round), certainty, Fear of nmitment, servedness, -man's land, sitation, biguity, pansionism.	Responsibility, Supportiveness, Kindliness, Care, Practicality, Abortive relationships, Mis-trust, Irresponsibility, Capriciousness, Hedonism, Civil servant syndrome (need to offload ultimate responsibility), Impracticality, Jealousy, Martyr, Sadism, Torpor, Reversion, Acquisitiveness, Slanderer.	Freedom, Laughter, Openness, Groundedness, Receptivity, Extreme laziness or activity, Self-protection, Self-preservation.

6 Motivation

You have control over action alone,
Never over its fruits.
Live not for the fruits of action,
Nor attach yourself to inaction.

BHAGAVAD GITA[19]

Let us look again at our house and now imagine it having many different rooms, the doors of which are labelled: physical handicap, mental retardedness, behavioural problems, emotional trauma, psychic possession and so on. This house can be compared to a person who suffers from one or some of these difficulties. Normally he is helped by a doctor, therapist or healer who goes into one of the rooms, and dealing more or less efficiently with the problem, gives the room a "spring clean". Healing, of whatever nature, takes place in the room, although it will be limited by the expertise of the practitioner or by the actual scope of the treatment. Allowing for these limitations, whatever form the treatment takes, it is obviously of great value as it helps alleviate the symptoms, the pain and the intensity of the illness.

As practitioners of the Metamorphic Technique, we work in a different way. We do not go into the house at all. Rather we stay at the front door and wedge it open, so we may observe the house as a whole and not as a collection of rooms; the air within the house then has a chance to renew itself, for all the rooms to have a thorough airing. In this way the fresh air, or the life force, can restore balance and harmony throughout the building and not just in one particular room. As practitioners, we do not direct or coerce the life force into doing anything; we do not impose a particular way upon it. Instead we stand back so that it can do exactly what it knows is necessary.

Our standing at the door is, in other words, the loosening of a time structure. All the characteristics we are working with are holds in time, so by focusing on the time when they were established, they can be dissolved along with everything that has since accrued to them.

The dissolution of these holds is accomplished by the life force of the patient. Life is not bound by time, space or matter, so the work can be done "out of time", and this is the uniqueness of the practice. For this reason it is essential for the practitioner to be "out of the way". If he is involved in the work then it cannot take place "out of time", it becomes just another form of therapy. To avoid this it is important to look at the motivation of the practitioner.

To be motivated is to have or impose a direction. The desire of a therapist or healer to cure will direct the patient's energy towards alleviating his ailments. This is as true of the doctor prescribing pills as it is of the healer seeing himself as a "channel" for divine energy. The symptoms are dealt with, in a more or less refined way. This is a normal and understandable approach, for when a patient comes to a practitioner, he usually comes with a reason in mind: he wants a cure for a physical disorder, perhaps he has a mental problem or he is under stress. He wants help for his problem, so treatment is aimed at relief, and that can be achieved. The cause of the trouble can also be relieved, but the responsibility of the patient in creating it is still there.

He has had very little to do with the healing, except for the desire to get better. He may unconsciously recreate the problem in some other way until the message that the body is showing through the symptoms is understood and the purpose of the particular ailment is realised. This re-creation of the problem can happen when the healing is done for the patient and not by him.

In the Metamorphic Technique our purpose is not to focus on particular problems, we are concerned with the patient as a whole. We may be aware of the symptoms or influences, but we know that they are there merely to reveal a blockage of energy. We do not attempt to decide what the patient needs or how we can help him. Our understanding of his problem can only come from our own mind which is just as limited as his so any help we may want to give will also have limitations. If we want to make someone better, we cannot help having an idea, conscious or unconscious, of what it would be like to be well. Yet in doing that we would restrict the patient's movement towards good health to what we understand that good health to be.

If we are motivated, if we seek to unblock or impose a direction on the patient's energy flow, if we think we know what the patient needs, then we are effectively coercing his life force to do what we feel is right for him. The question is, how can we know what is right? How can we have a better idea than the patient's own life force of the change that is necessary for him? Practitioner and patient alike are both limited to the confines of their understanding. A practitioner, however expert, can never truly know what is right, only the life force of the patient knows.

There is some difficulty in understanding this. During a treatment, whatever it may be, the patient is in a vulnerable position where he can be easily influenced. The practitioner has certain ideas about the patient's condition and may exercise his will. An ailment or energy block can be cured, but possibly at the price of interfering with the life process which, at its own pace, is quite capable of healing. That pace, rather than an imposed one, is absolutely right. It is even possible for the life force of the patient to directly resist the will of the practitioner, and an impasse, or even damage, may occur. From another angle, until we reach the state of ultimate perfection, we all have imperfections. To add our own to those of another may bring about a cure but will not make for perfection, other imperfections will become manifest.

So in the Metamorphic Technique, the practitioners do not impose a direction. The patient's life is his own and he must be allowed the space in which to take full responsibility for himself. It is only he who can discover, if necessary, the purpose behind his own energy blocks. This responsibility need not be seen as a "duty" but as an ability to respond, both to ourselves and to the world. When we realise that we are fully responsible for who and what we are from the moment of conception onwards, and are able to respond more fully, then our ability to heal ourselves comes a step nearer.

The practitioner, without motivation, is a catalyst. The more uninvolved he is, the better catalyst he will be. It is the same as the way in which the earth is a catalyst for a seed. The earth is totally unconcerned with what the seed is or when the plant is going to emerge, but it acts as a catalyst that this may happen. The power within the seed releases the potential of the plant to grow, to develop and blossom according to its own inner programming. The seed uses the earth in its own time, at its own pace. The earth does not create the plant, it allows the power within the seed to make use of it. The growth of the seed is thus from the centre out, it is not imposed upon by the earth.

As the earth has no motive, so the practitioner in the Metamorphic Technique has no motive; he is merely a catalyst with no desire to help, heal or influence the patient. The patient's life force will indicate the changes it knows to be necessary, the changes coming from within. His vital energy, his passion for life, all that is entailed in being human, will work to bring about the change to ensure in him balance and wholeness. Like the seed, the patient also has the potential for growth and that growth is unique to himself, it cannot be known by another. As the earth meets the needs of the seed by just being there, so the practitioner meets the needs of the patient's life force by just being there. He is not imposing anything, he is simply focusing onto the life force while he massages the feet. Life has a direction of growth, of expansion, and is of infinite potential, eager to become actual. So we can see how important it is for the practitioner to be clear about his motivation.

Many of us spend our time looking for the cause of our problems through therapy, analysis or even spiritual healing. By considering cause and effect in this way, we put ourselves in a world of symptoms and reasons, and yet more reasons, a world concerned with matter and the limitations of matter. Whether we consider the cause or the effect, we are caught in a never ending circuit.

The prenatal pattern stretches beyond cause and effect, beyond matter, time and space, to before conception. There, it is proposed, life first began to attract to itself the various influences that were later precipitated into matter. These influences may result in manifestations that range from mental retardedness to genius, from emotional peaks to the lowest depths, from being accident prone to having fine physical energy. But we are not directly concerned with them, ruled as they are by the law of cause and effect; we look to the purpose beyond and to the potential they help realise. This potential is one of being without blocks, of not being governed by holds in time or by influences laid down in the past. It is a potential of greater awareness, of higher evolution. The consciousness of the practitioner acts as a bridge, as it were, between what is out of time, our full potential, and what is in time, our present state.

To be without motivation implies detachment, but this does not mean that the practitioner is cold or uncaring. He is aware of the movement of energy within the patients, the symptoms, ailments and problems, and may be filled with empathy for the suffering that they are experiencing. But he is not primarily concerned with that suffering, rather with the life beyond it. One of the meanings of the word detachment is to "send on a mission". In this sense, the practitioner is seeing the patient off on his own mission, knowing that the patient's life force will direct aright.

As the earth is indifferent to the seed, so the

practitioner is working with indifference towards the ailments or difficulties of the patient. Indifference here means one without difference or inclination, not inclined to prefer one thing to another, neutral. However, intrinsic to our nature is a caring quality established in us even before birth. During the post-conception period, our formative time, we were establishing our individuality along with our commitment to life. The driving force behind this commitment is our passion for life. During the pre-birth period we opened ourselves to the world around us, exploring our environment and preparing ourselves for our future relationships with people and the nature kingdoms. The passion for life is expressed here as com-passion, a feeling of at-onement with others. So the practitioner, knowing that he is compassion, shares his own passion for life with the passion for life within the patient.

These qualities of detachment and compassion can be seen in parents as they watch their child learning to walk. The child will get up, try to walk and fall down many times. If they always rush to help, he will never learn to do it for himself. The child has the ability to walk and the parents know this; they also know they must let him learn in his own way even though they long to help. They stand aside and remain detached whilst being filled with love and compassion. The impulse to help is real and valid. However, in non-action, true help is given.

This attitude of non-interference is often confusing, as whenever we touch another person physically, there is an exchange of energy, and this also happens when we massage a patient's feet. Therefore we could say that the practitioner is bound to be affecting the patient directly through physical contact. This may well be true but remember the attitude of mind of the practitioner. The important difference is that the practitioner is not *trying* to heal the patient, is not using magnetic energy as a means of healing. Physical healing may take place as a result of the treatment, as it would in Reflexology, but this is a fringe benefit. The real purpose of the treatment is to go beyond all levels, including the physical.

When we massage a foot, we point through the stepped down energy to the highest reality there is, to life itself. We are working with time and timelessness, and the healing occurs because the patient is no longer subject to the holds in time. The fact that there is life is the only requirement for this. No matter how deep the realisation goes, it does not alter the importance of this one requirement. If we refer back to our house built with a faulty nail in its structure, we could say that we are pointing to the moment in time when the faulty nail was put in, for behind the fault lies the image of the perfect structure.

We have assumed that for life to manifest as a human being, there has to be a blueprint for man, materials and influences that go into the making of a unique individual, through whom a unique purpose will be fulfilled. If we had remained at the stage of the blueprint, nothing in the universe would have been gained. For evolution to take place we have to let that purpose enact itself in matter through us. This is why it is so important for the practitioner not to interfere with the process. As he lets life act for the patient, the patient is able to move on from the knowledge that he *has* life to the realisation that he *is* life.

It is not necessary for us to know much about this practice. It has been noticed that it is enough at times for just one person in the room to be aware of its higher implications, and because this bridge of consciousness is present, the life force will release the blocks without impediments. This is illustrated in the story of a mentally retarded adolescent. The boy had spent much of his life by the sea, often walking barefoot on a pebbled beach. His mother heard of the Metamorphic Technique and took a training. After three months of foot massage, she expressed her astonishment at the beneficial changes. "Why," she wondered, "had the massage indicated this change, when walking on the beach, which after all, was a form of massage, had not done so?" The difference was that consciousness was now at work, through the expanded awareness of the mother due to her training and practice.

So we have to look closely at our own motivation in this work. How detached can we be? There are bound to be times when we long to help someone, when our feelings of compassion for a crippled child overwhelm us, when we hear a story of intense suffering that urges us to try to heal. Sickness and pain surround us and anyone with any feelings will want to help in some way. But the truest help we can give is that of non-interference, as we recognise that the healing takes place from within, that the life force will do what is necessary even if it does not appear to be right at the time. Each of us is unique, we each have our own path to follow, and our life force must be given the space in which we can do this.

7 Manifestations of Change

What we call the beginning is often the end
And to make an end is to make a beginning

T. S. ELIOT[20]

When we fall ill and go to a doctor or therapist, we are probably hoping for immediate results, for a change to take place that is observable physically (if the illness is a physical one), for someone who will release our tension so we can get some sleep, for someone to soothe our distraught emotions. Because of this "results syndrome", we look for outside help and want it to work instantly; we want results. Sadly, over the years, we have largely lost the ability to be responsible for our own state of health, and have put that responsibility onto people we do not even know. We are relieved if it works but are frustrated, and go elsewhere if it does not. Most of the time we are out of contact with our inner selves. We prefer to remain so rather than re-establish contact, and prevent the purpose of the illness from becoming clear. We may be temporarily cured but after a time the energy block will reappear, perhaps in some other form.

The person involved, however, can make a deliberate choice to free himself. He can act in order to seek help, in the knowledge of what is taking place. When we begin to take responsibility for ourselves, we see results in a very different light. As changes begin to manifest, we recognise what the bodymind is saying, we understand why we are ill and why the energy blocks are there, and we stop suppressing them, as a surfer rides the waves instead of battling against them. In the Metamorphic Technique we find that all forms of dis-ease are highlighting a blocking of energy, and when the energy flow is freed, the dis-ease is resolved. The healing may take time to become apparent, results may not be immediate, but they tend to be permanent.

Inner changes are usually recognised as a subtle reorientation, a growing sense of purpose, a new direction, a sense of "getting on course", a feeling of rightness. A patient has written to us: "I feel a dropping away of old patterns. When confronted with familiar situations, I find I'm just about to respond in my normal manner when something stops me. A voice inside says, wait a minute, that's the old pattern, what's the new one? Then I find I'm responding in a different way; a new pattern is emerging." Sometimes there are very definite changes one can see or feel, as a four year old girl who walked for the first time in her life after only a few treatments, but often the changes are intangible, the energy is moving on so deep a level that we are almost unaware of it. It is like trying to watch a plant grow — we know it is growing but we cannot actually see it happening. We may not be able to relate, for instance, the fact that we have got a new job, a house, or a lover with the fact that we are having our feet massaged every week. Friends say they see the difference in us but we find it hard to believe them. We are not aware of the changes because they come from within and we are those changes. We cannot measure them against something that is fixed as everything in us is in a state of flux. Furthermore, we sometimes even lose the memory of how we used to be, and the problems that we battled against.

It is never possible to define the nature of the change, the time it will take, or the manner in which it will happen. Can the ways of life ever be defined? The impetus, the movement of change, comes from the life force, and so it will contrive circumstances or "co-incidences" that cannot be explained, in order to effect a release. Anything, from a chance encounter, a bad fall, a sudden fever, or a different therapy may be used when and if they are needed, to bring about a state of wholeness. The life force will engineer this so that the inner healing will take place. One patient who had a bad back had seen many different osteopaths before coming regularly to have his feet massaged. He then met a new osteopath, and after manipulation the pain in his back was relieved. The life force used the help of this osteopath to release the energy, but the back did not get better solely because of the manipulation. It improved because the pain was no longer necessary — as the patient was having his feet massaged, the life force had started activating the learning and healing process.

Although momentous changes may take place, we have noticed that at no time is the patient unable to cope with the changes, a state of balance is always maintained. The life force is regulating the inner movement, and it ensures that nothing detrimental will happen. Of course we cannot say specifically what the life force will or will not do, but the mechanics at work appear to sustain an equilibrium even when deep hidden patterns come to the surface and are released. A state of inner rightness and stability under-lies the movement of change.

This applies when what is known as the Law of Cure or Regression occurs, where we appear to get worse, or may even experience past illnesses or difficulties. In the Metamorphic Technique, as we are working on loosening a time structure, the past is being brought into focus and the holds in time let go. It is not however always necessary for the past to come into full consciousness, as the release is in the abstract; it is the energy that was diverted by the events of the past that is being dealt with, rather than the events themselves. It may be that we do actually experience these events but they will be of much shorter duration, with greater or less intensity. It is the life force that is effecting the regression, and, however difficult the changes may be, they always take place at the right time, and with sufficient energy.

One example of this regression is when children, even though they are 5 or 6 years old, will regress to a stage of 3 or 4 months. When this happens, the parents should respond accordingly. A child of a few months old needs a great deal of loving physical contact, so if the parents understand, and respond as though he were actually a baby, he will feel the security he needs, and will be able to move forward again.

As we change our environment changes, and this affects those around us. This can be seen clearly in the case of Mary, a woman in her early forties who had suffered from severe depression for many years. Separated from her husband, with three children, she was living with a friend who was in a similar situation with two children. Mary had reached the point of being referred to a psychiatrist, becoming totally isolated and agoraphobic. She began to receive the

Metamorphic massage, and a few months later she decided that what she really wanted to do was to go to bed, to opt out completely and spend time alone. In her own words, it was the hardest thing she had ever done. There was tremendous resistance because of her responsibilities, but to her surprise, the whole household rallied round to support her. She eventually spent 5 weeks in bed and like a baby alternately cried a great deal or lay and did nothing. Vivid dreams followed, mostly indicating a conflict in her finding her own identity, especially as a woman. Throughout her time in bed, she continued to have her feet massaged regularly. When she eventually got up she felt renewed, released. She took up painting, and got a job as an assistant physiotherapist in a psychiatric ward. It had been a time of "coming back to a state of non-struggle, a coming into a knowledge of self."

Mary's story shows a regression taking place to allow for a movement forward, but it also shows how the environment came to accommodate the changes happening in her. Where Mary took responsibility, others carried on with it, and in so doing discovered new areas in themselves.

Transformation is not an easy process. As we let go of our old patterns, our fears and inferiorities, we open the way to move on — forwards and upwards — to new patterns, new understandings and expansion. But there can be a tremendous resistance to letting go; memories from the past hold us back as much as fear of the future. A person who has suffered an acute disability for many years, will have grown accustomed to it, it has become a normal condition; unconsciously, there might be the feeling of fear of being free. People who undertake to have the Metamorphic massage, and are beginning to change, may suddenly stop having the treatment for a while. This may be due to a deeply rooted unconscious fear of change, of losing control, of letting go what is familiar, and having to move into unknown ground.

There are also times when a person seems, consciously or not, actually to prevent himself from allowing anything to happen. When this happens the feet that are being massaged can feel heavy, lifeless, physical extensions that do not belong to the body above. It is a paradoxical situation, as if the door to the patient's life force has been opened and then slammed shut again. Nevertheless the fact that he has come to receive the massage means that there is an overall desire for change.

With this Technique, the life force is healing from within us, so any form of illness can be looked on as "curable". At times a serious degenerate condition may not alter directly, but the attitude of mind behind the condition can change and this is what can affect us physically. Mental retardedness and brain damage are both conditions that have been known to change considerably, especially with children, as their patterns are not yet fixed as are those of adults. Children are freer; it is easier for them to change.

Practitioners working with patients with such conditions as Down's syndrome and autism, say how they notice first a sparkle coming to the children's eyes, and this is followed by a greater awareness and mobility. It would appear that a child suffering from Down's syndrome is in this condition because of his eagerness to incarnate, so he works his way out of the syndrome by going through the stages of development that he missed. Conversely, an autistic child seems to be so because of a reluctance to come into matter and change will be effected by his coming more into contact with reality.

When we have received a Metamorphic treatment, we often have a feeling of energy flowing, a new vibration within the bodymind, a landscape, as it were, opening up within. As we let go we gain far more than we lose. As Mary once said: "I felt that my awareness was being stretched, that I was both dislocated and delighted at the same time." But we may also experience a feeling of confusion as the energy shifts and begins to find a new expression. It can take a day or two to settle down. After spring cleaning a room that has been in the same condition for 40 years, we need to re-orientate ourselves in our new environment. Some of the objects will have been changed around and others discarded. It takes a little time to feel at home again. If we move the furniture around too often, we have no chance to live in the room and appreciate it. This need for time to settle down is the major reason why we treat adults for one hour only once a week. More often than that can result in confusion. The patient uses the time in between each massage to re-orientate and get accustomed to the new inner environment.

Time is an indefineable concept. With the Metamorphic Technique the work is done "out of time", although the energy is released in time. The life force of the patient may take weeks or months to bring about a transformation. So, when one is asked how long it will take for change to come along, the answer can not be given. By our taking responsibility for our own healing, our life force has the space and the time in which to move.

8 Patients and Practitioners

Your children are not your children,
They are the sons and daughters of Life's longing for itself

KAHLIL GIBRAN[21]

The word patient means "one who is suffering"; we suffer from the restrictions of having come into matter with a limited mind, power and consciousness. In this sense, we are all patients. We can learn the Metamorphic Technique and be both patients and practitioners for each other, even though we may know very little about the principles behind the work. It is through both giving and receiving a massage that we learn about it most. The practice speaks louder and clearer than this book can ever do.

The simplicity of the Technique, which is outlined in the next chapter, is its beauty. There is no mystique about it, no need for years of training, no examination in order to qualify. What we do is to focus on the life force by using the feet as a support in matter for a time structure. The patient's own inner healing power takes over and operates without interference. A simple yet dynamic process.

Massaging one another has proved to be especially important within the context of a family, whose members will be changing together. As one member of the family is being treated, the patterns and characteristics of the family as one living unit may come to the surface. Every member reflects another, so if one member is undergoing change, all will be affected in a roundabout way. But if there is a reluctance to that movement of change within the family, then the work of transformation will be more difficult and the massage may even come to an end. For this reason it is important for the whole family to be involved in the physical giving and receiving of the treatment. From experience we have learned that the family unit can move and grow as a whole if there is this total involvement.

Time and again it has been observed that parents are the best practitioners for their children, and vice versa. This may seem strange as parents could find it hardest to be detached, especially if their child is in any way handicapped. They are obviously desirous for change to take place; but as parents have so close a link with their children genetically, they have an intuitive knowledge of the child's genetic pattern, and when they touch its feet they are literally contacting their own building bricks; their fingers are directed by the knowledge supplied by their own cells, and this applies also to children working on their parents' feet. As well as the genetic links, we must assume that there are also other deep links, for the same type of response occurs between parents and their adopted children, and also between partners in a close relationship. With children having the Metamorphic massage, especially those mentally retarded, when the father starts having his feet massaged as well, there is often a great leap forward in the child's development. The same happens when the father starts working on his child's feet. Why this is so we cannot say, except to suggest that the reason may be the father's greater involvement with his family; or because of the correspondence between the father principle and the moment of conception when conditions such as mental retardedness were established.

The mother of a Down's syndrome baby, on hearing of the Metamorphic Technique, came to us to train and showed her husband how to give the massage. They started a routine of working with their child every day for ten minutes; while the mother fed her, the father massaged her feet. They had decided not to have another child through fear that it might also be handicapped. However after a year of treatment they became confident that even if a second child were to be mentally retarded, they now had the means to help reverse the situation. The little girl has now developed so much that she is going to primary school, and the parents have had another child.

It often happens that parents prefer to pass on the responsibility for their child to a practitioner. Even though it is pointed out that the movement of change would be greater if they too received the massage, they say there is nothing wrong with them, and express great reluctance to be treated or to treat each other. As we have seen, parents and children reflect one another. If a child is changing but there is resistance in his family, he will experience conflict within him because his environment no longer reflects who he is. His life force may then create a new situation in which he will be removed from the family for a while. It may be that the child receives an invitation for a few weeks' holiday; perhaps he gets a sudden fever that the doctors cannot explain and he is taken into hospital for observation. This space of time gives the child the opportunity to gain strength and independence, and so to find his own direction. The parents are able to rest and re-orientate themselves, so that when the child returns home it is to a new-found balance within the family. This exemplifies how vital it is that the whole family should be involved.

When a family first comes to this work, there is often a great enthusiasm and a desire to start immediately. Then after a time, even though a change is taking place, especially in the child, the parents' interest wanes and eventually the treatments are stopped. Many excuses will be made such as not having the time, or not knowing how to do the massage properly. What is really going on is a resistance to change. There was the sad case of a four year old boy who psychologically would not talk although physically he was quite able to do so. After five treatments the boy said "thank you" to the practitioner, and from that time he started to talk. Then, unexpectedly, his mother decided to stop the treatments. It was clear that she was resistant to the change in her child and to any resulting changes in herself. She also resented the fact that the practitioner was the one her child was focusing on but still she would not do the massage herself.

This type of situation is not at all uncommon. Parents usually adapt to the retardedness in their child and centre their lives around it. They are not able to cope with any change in themselves that their changing child now demands of them. Consequently when parents take their child to a practitioner, it is advisable to massage the parents first, then encourage them to work with the child. In most therapies, parents are not to be involved, because they are considered to be a part of the problem, but with us they are asked to be involved precisely because they may be part of the solution to the problem. The child has been attracted to his parents as the providers of the ideal environment for his growth and learning, and because the whole family has something to learn from each other.

A couple, with some reluctance lest their hopes should be ill-founded, brought their epileptic daughter to a practitioner, and were surprised to find that they were to receive the massage first. The father declined, but when he saw his wife become very relaxed after ten minutes he relented. They were then shown how to massage the child and he began to realise the importance of his own involvement. As the practitioner made no claims to a cure, they understood that it was their daughter's own life force that would bring about changes in her. They learned how essential it was for them to do the massage, both with the child and with each other. As they left the mother remarked that if nothing else, at least they had been shown that there was something positive they could do, in place of their helplessness.

In conditions such as mental retardedness, the parents often feel tremendous guilt; some parents think that their child's illness has been "sent by God" and they have no right to interfere. But while there is life in the child, there is the possibility of change; he has the potential of wholeness, and for that reason the parents should not feel they have to accept the situation, and not attempt to be catalysts so that the situation may be revised by their child's life force. That one child in the family should have recessive genes and the other children do not, is part of the law that each person "chooses", and attracts to himself, his own reality, in this case it is mental retardedness. It cannot be considered as the "fault" of the parents or "God's wish". To take responsibility for ourselves is one of the prerogatives of being human. So what the parents can do is to help the child through the massage, to come closer to realising the purpose behind his handicap.

Life begins at conception, so it is possible to treat a pregnant woman, both for the embryo and for herself. For the embryo, the massage may come through the mother. This will enable it to be free of the influences precipitated at conception before they actually come into form, and will give confidence to emerge into the world. It will be able to move through the birth process more easily. It appears that often a difficult birth is caused more by resistance in the child to being born than by any weakness in the mother. It is thought that the embryo influences the mother on every level throughout her pregnancy, so if she has her feet done regularly characteristics such as cravings or depressive states, can be eased. Through the massage she will find herself becoming more free of her difficulties, including the fear of giving birth.

During labour the massage can be of tremendous help. Often there can be unexpected tensions and panic, feelings of inadequacy, and reluctance to go through with the birth. The massage can loosen these tensions, but the mother must indicate where she wants it — on the feet, the hands or the head — as the coming baby may be blocking off the action of any one of her centres, the moving, doing or thinking centre. Only five minutes will help, and the mother will derive the greatest benefit if the massage is done by the father.

When a baby is born he can be massaged straight away without any risk. The patterns formed during the gestation period will be dissolved before they become fixed. This release of energy will help the baby to grow in a balanced and unrestricted way. There may be more ease of movement throughout life, more awareness and openness to change. The massage loosens the patterns from the past and opens the way for the future, and of course the younger a child is the more easily this will happen.

The question is always asked: can one treat oneself? Yes, this is possible, and is certainly advisable if there is no one else to do it. But in giving the massage to oneself, it is possible to create a 'closed circuit', as it were, in which blocked energies may be retained. It is easy to become involved with one's own symptoms as the fingers find, with great accuracy, points of tension on the feet, and any such self-involvement makes it difficult to be detached. It can be helpful to use a vibrator, as this mechanical aid is not involved as one is oneself. But although the vibrator acts as a third party, it is still not impartial to the blocked energies. At times it will stick on a point or over-heat, as the concentration of energy affects it. To overcome this, or if you have not got a vibrator, to break free of the closed circuit, you can imagine a ball of light within yourself, radiating outwards. Send the energy off into the cosmos on the rays of the light.

The closed circuit principle can also apply to a family, the released energies may stay within that living unit for some time. And so it is best if from time to time one member receives a massage from an outside practitioner, breaking the circuit. If someone realises that the family, or one individual in it, is motivated and is trying to achieve results or bring about changes at all cost, then it is important to suggest that a practitioner steps in for a while so that equilibrium may be preserved.

9 The Practice

*The pressure of the hands causes
the springs of life to flow.*

TOKUJIRO NANIKOSHI[22]

From the appearance on earth of *homo erectus* to man as a civilised being, his journey can be traced historically. This development was possible because of his ability to change, movement being the underlying factor at work in the evolution of the universe. Thinking, as we humans perform that action, is a fairly recent attribute, together with the ability to create things. Beyond his intellect and his creative powers, man yearns for something more. This yearning stimulates his intellect to reach out towards the universal mind and propel him into the upper reaches of knowledge.

So in the Metamorphic Technique, we work mainly on the feet as corresponding to that essential quality of movement. Our movement forward in the world is with our feet, and we start the practice there, then we move on to the hands and the head.

The Treatment

You can treat wherever you are, at any time of day. There are no special requirements. The patient may be watching television, reading a book, or simply doing nothing. You can do the feet of a person in bed, and if he falls asleep then just carry on until the treatment is completed. Some people like to talk, others go into a deep relaxation, it makes no difference. But if you are talking with a patient, be careful not to get involved in diagnosis, let your hands get on with the massage while you remain detached. The state of the patient makes no difference to the treatment.

Anyone can massage another person. A child can treat his parents, a grandmother her grandson, one can work with one's friends and with complete strangers. A mentally retarded child can rub your feet just as you can rub his. It is the life and the intelligence inherent in each person that is at work.

The Feet

Firstly, sit at right angles to your patient, with his right foot comfortably in your lap *(See Fig 9)*. You can use a small cloth under his foot. The practitioner sits in this position to convey his attitude that he is "out of the way" of the patient. Sitting opposite to him would make it difficult to remain uninvolved.

9   *Position for the practice.*

Place your hands over the foot and pause for a moment before you take hold of it, giving yourself the time to become centred, to leave behind the thoughts of the day, and allow the patient time to adjust to your presence. It is a moment of focusing.

Then take the foot firmly with both hands and begin to get acquainted with it, let your hands roam freely for a few minutes over the foot and the ankle. Having a firm touch does away with any feelings of ticklishness, which is merely superficial tension. You are working not only with the foot but with the whole person, so let your consciousness be informed of the condition of the foot, the hard and soft tissues and the fluids, as a portrayal of the overall state of being. Notice if the foot is cold, moist or dry, fleshy or skinny, flexible or rigid. Feel whether the skin is smooth or rough; look to see if there are any callosities and if so, where they are situated. Feel the different bones throughout the foot. Notice all of this, acknowledge it, and then let it go. You are not diagnosing or thinking of changing anything. You simply observe, think no more about it and move on. By gently massaging the whole foot you are acknowledging the patient in his totality.

From here, begin the massage by using your thumbs and fingers up and down the spinal reflexes from the big toe to the heel *(See Fig* 10*)*. Imagine a medial line along the bony ridge on the inside of the foot. Allow your fingers to go along this line wherever they want to. The intelligence in your fingers is far more in tune with what needs to be done than your mind is, so let them be your guide. Use any fingers you want, with any movement or pressure you feel comfortable with. The movement can, for instance, be circular, probing, or vibratory, as if you were playing a tiny 'cello. You may find the pressure going from very light to quite firm, different fingers coming into use at different times. Just do whatever feels right.

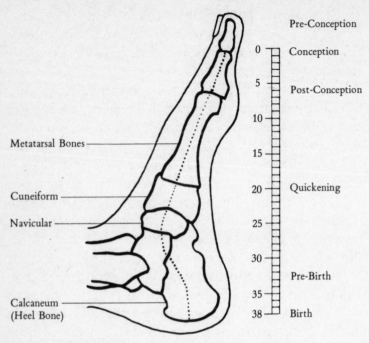

Pre-Conception

0 — Conception

5 — Post-Conception

10

Metatarsal Bones — 15

Cuneiform — 20 — Quickening

Navicular — 25

30

Calcaneum — 35 Pre-Birth
(Heel Bone) 38 — Birth

10 *Chart of the foot relating to the prenatal pattern.*

Work all over the outside edge of the big toe, paying attention to the upper and lower corners of the nail, the reflex points of the pineal and pituitary glands. Then from the joint of the big toe, the reflex point of conception, follow the bony ridge down along the arch. Notice the groove between the internal cuneiform and the navicular bones, as on the chart, which corresponds to the period of quickening. Move onto the calcaneum under the ankle and massage the whole of the side of the heel area to the point where the Achilles tendon is inserted. Here is the birth reflex point. Work only on the bone and, at the heel, on the padded area to the side, where it is difficult at times to feel the bone.

Occasionally work from under the inner ankle bone, across the top of the foot, to under the outer ankle bone. This is the reflex area of the pelvic girdle, which corresponds to the centre of movement within the body and in terms of consciousness, to the principle of action.

As you do the massage, the patient may well say that some areas are more painful than others, or you may notice that some areas feel sticky or blocked. Just acknowledge this and then let the knowledge go. Do not purposefully work on these areas more than others, nor should you avoid them. Treat the whole foot in the same way. Reassure the patient that he need not worry if his feet go to sleep! This is usually just due to lack of circulation.

Having worked for 30 minutes, stroke the foot all over to finish. You can work with your hands a little away from the foot, without touching it, for a few minutes if you want to, following along the bony ridge.

Then use the same procedure on the other foot. After both feet have been massaged, wash your hands in cold water which does not open the pores, to remove any excess energy you may have picked up from the patient.

The Hands

Begin in the same way as you did for the feet, centring yourself over the right hand before you actually take hold of it. The pattern you follow is from the top of the thumb down the outside edge, always along the bony ridge, to the wrist *(See Fig 11)*. Massage across the

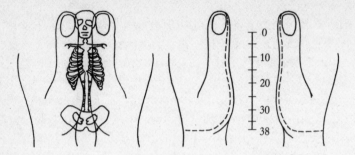

11   *Chart of the hands.*

back of the wrist occasionally as you did across the ankle. From the right hand go on to the left.

Do both hands for 5-10 minutes, or longer if the patient wishes.

The Head

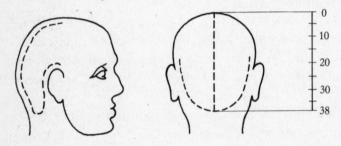

12   *Chart of the head.*

Let the patient sit in a chair and stand behind him. Centre yourself, holding your hands above his head for a few moments. Then massage up and down from the top of the head to the base of the skull along a central medial line *(See Fig 12)*. Use one hand for the massage and rest the other lightly on the forehead to support the head, this saves the neck muscles from tensing. Lift the fingers as you work from one point to another so they do not pull the hair. The touch can be very gentle. Massage also along the base of the skull, following the occipital ridge up to the mastoid bones, then behind and up to the top of the ears. This area reflects the pelvic girdle. Use either both hands for this, or one hand at a time. Feel free, allow your hands to tell you what to do.

The head can be massaged for 10 minutes or longer. The patient usually feels happily relaxed, so do not disturb him, leave him alone for a few minutes while you wash your hands in cold water. After any massage, allow your patient time and space to be quiet, if he so wishes.

Right/Left

Normally the massage starts with the right foot or hand and then goes on to the left side.

The right represents what the patient is working with in his life now, it shows what he is making of his life. The left expresses the dormant and potential patterns, those that he came into life with but are at the moment held in suspense. By starting on the right side, the life force seems to clear the way for the other patterns to be released.

Occasionally, especially with children, a patient may ask you to do the left foot first, as if their life force is indicating that the more hidden patterns are to be worked on immediately. If this is the case, go along with what they want. They are usually quite happy to let you have the right foot afterwards, so do not impose any "right foot, left foot" procedure.

Try, if possible, to get both feet done in one treatment so there is no lop-sidedness!

How long, how often?

It is important not to give an adult more than an hour's treatment on their feet per week, that is, half an hour on each foot. More than that and some chaos or confusion may ensue as the inner "furniture" is moved too quickly. It is essential for the patient to have time to re-orientate himself between treatments. To do the massage too often would be an imposition on the natural pace of the life force, and would create imbalance. The only exception to this is at times of crisis, when the hour of massage can be prolonged and done through the week, with ten minutes at the most per day on each foot. The massage can of course be spread out through the week for anyone.

With children it is different. They are moving at a much faster pace within themselves, so can cope easily with more frequent treatments. It is difficult for a child to sit still for very long, so they can be treated every few days, or even every day, for a few minutes at a time. Here it is obviously better if the child's parents do the massage. One Down's syndrome child whom we know loves having her feet done so much that she sticks them out of bed before going to sleep each night. She is quite happy to go without a drink or a story but will complain bitterly if her feet are not rubbed.

The hands and the head can be massaged as often and for as long a time as the patient wishes. The hands and the head are expressions of the secondary functions — doing and thinking — so the effect of the massage is not so far-reaching as on the feet. The feet, on the other hand, express the primary function of the universe — movement — so massage has a much greater effect and there is the possibility it could be overdone.

We can see therefore that the actual treatment is very easy to do: a simple massage of the spinal reflexes along the inner bony ridges of the feet and ankles, the hands and wrists, along the centre line of the skull and up to the ears. For how long the treatments should be given is more difficult to say, only the patient can really know. He may want one treatment, he may wish to continue for several weeks or months. Start off once a week and wait and see. The patient may decide to come for a number of consecutive weeks, and then come every other week, or once a month. The life force within him knows what he needs and he must have the space in which to make his own decisions. So if a patient suddenly decides to stop being treated or doesn't turn up for his appointment, do not press him. It may be that his life force is saying he has had enough for now, is not ready or able to cope with more. Patients choose their practitioner and regulate the frequency of their visits, through discovering and exercising their own inner authority.

The practitioner

While giving a treatment certain symptomatic conditions can arise within you and it is good to be prepared for them, and know how to cope. They are not important in themselves, they are simply manifestations of energy coming from the patient through you; but if they are not released you may experience slight headaches, nausea or fatigue. The following are the sort of conditions that may occur:

1. Your fingers or hands begin to feel very heavy, like lead. They may also get hot or there may be

throbbing sensations. If this happens, give your hands a good shake and wash them in cold water, as usual, immediately after the treatment.

2. A feeling of general fatigue. This is especially common in treating mentally retarded people, or one's own children, as they very willingly release their blocked energy. Here there is a need to be centred so you can throw off the fatigue. It can help to picture pure white light radiating from your heart, filling your whole body, until you are a ball of light. Radiate the light outwards and send the energy off on the light rays so it cannot stay in your body making you feel tired.

Use the same procedure if you experience a slight pain anywhere in your body. Do not worry about it as it is not your pain. Send it away on the light.

3. Yawning, coughing, burping, sneezing, sighing: do not stifle these actions, rather encourage or even exaggerate them. Really yawn — apologise to your patient if you wish and assure him you are not really all that tired! This frees you of the energy you have picked up.

The Conceptual Pattern

An extension of the work on the prenatal pattern is that on the conceptual pattern, where we work only on the area just above the conception point.

Before conception, everything that we are going to be is there in the abstract. By massaging that area we are focusing on what is about to be created but has not yet come into matter. The life force can directly affect the incoming influences, allowing us to move forward without these influences having to be precipitated. We are however, in time and these influences are already manifest.

Because we are now working out of time, in pre-conception, the purpose for the holds in time can be seen; their need to be established becomes irrelevant. In this way our blueprint is revised and more fully perfected.

As there is no involvement with matter and time, we can work on this area as often as we like, and for as long as we like. We must also go on massaging the prenatal pattern as we are in matter and our characteristics have materialised.

We can use the conceptual pattern work on ourselves, on others, or on those who are not with us. The area involved is found above the first joints of the big toes or thumbs, and on the top of the head centrally. We can just hold or use a slight vibratory movement *(See Fig 13)*.

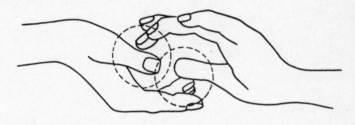

13   *The conceptual pattern.*

Another way of doing it, for oneself or for another who is absent, is by putting one of our hands on top of the other, palms together but fingers facing in opposite directions. We then slide our hands apart until one of the fingers on each hand touches the point just above the first knuckle on each thumb, on the outer edge, or on the pineal or pituitary reflex points. In doing this we are creating an open-ended circuit of energy. To work on ourselves, we put our name in the circle, simply holding ourselves there for as long as we want. In working for others, we do the same thing only it is their name that is in the circle. As we are out of time, space and matter, the motivation aspect is not an issue. Our will can only be imposed upon what is already incarnated, not on what is as yet only potential. All the same, as a matter of course, we do not visualise the person being well, nor do we focus on the ailment or difficulty. We just put the absent person's name in the circuit and hold it there. We can put our family there, animals, the city or country we live in, the earth or the universe. We are focusing on the point before even the universe was created in matter, and we are focusing on that potential.

10 Conclusion

Every person,
All the events in your life
Are there because you have drawn them there.
What you choose
To do with them is
Up to you.

RICHARD BACH[21]

As the universe is constantly expanding, so our journey on earth is a journey of expansion. The first single cell grows into an embryo which, at 4-5 months, directs its consciousness away from itself to discover something other than self, purposefully exploring the environment of the womb. At birth we emerge into the world and begin to apprehend it with our senses, hands and toes. Eventually we start walking and this urge enables us to move further away from our parents so we may discover the world. As we grow and become conditioned, we have to expand in consciousness to go beyond that conditioning. We extend our frontiers, leaving home and reaching out to deeper understandings. We start to explore the universe with our minds and intuition.

The beginning of the journey is at conception, the fulfilment is expansion into the highest plane of existence. Throughout the journey we are totally responsible for who we are and who we become. Our choice is whether or not to take this responsibility and open ourselves to change, to evolution.

In the Metamorphic Technique, we are getting in

touch with the principles of life itself and the underlying universal laws. We find ourselves on the most
exciting and rewarding journey of all. Our conscious
holding on to a fixed image of ourselves is released,
and the higher mind within us is allowed the space
in which to take control. It is rarely a clear journey
or even an easy one. Again and again we find ourselves working blind, with the faith that the purpose
is being fulfilled, that integration is taking place even
when there appears to be disintegration. Being blind
demands total trust in the life force that it is doing what
is right for us.

Our feet are our channels of communication with
the earth and they hold one of the keys to the healing
and energising forces within us. We allow our fingers
to work on the feet, to go where they will, to explore,
probe, vibrate and rub. We acknowledge the higher
wisdom of the life force to bring about the changes we
need. All we do is loosen a time structure. If a gutter
pipe is blocked with leaves, it is no good pushing and
bashing at it. The easiest way is for water to be poured
through and for the pipe to be gently shaken. The
blockage will move. So life moves without force. As
long as there is life, our potential to flow freely can be
realised.

If we have attracted to ourselves certain characteristics, why do we want to change them? We do it so
we may see the deeper purpose beyond. We have the
choice of losing what we think we are and finding
ourselves beyond the influences that have created the
fabric of our self. We have the choice between being
stuck with our view of life or opening new vistas
within ourselves so we may see beyond. Nothing is

permanent, nothing is fixed, so it is up to us to take the responsibility for our own evolution and begin to reach beyond our limitations. Our potential is limitless and the choice is ours. However, the ultimate choice is up to life, and we are that life.

Bibliography

Ascent of Man, J. Bronowski, B.B.C. Publications, London,
    1973
Bioenergetics, A. Lowen, Penguin Books, London, 1975
Birth Without Violence, F. Leboyer, Faber, London, 1976
Bhagavad Gita, The, The Penguin Classics, Penguin Books, 1962
Bodymind, K. Dytchwold, Wildwood House, London, 1977
Dancing Wu Li Masters, G. Zukav, Rider, London, 1979
Four Quartets, T. S. Eliot, Faber, London
Grey's Anatomy, Bounty Books, New York
Magic Casements, G. Trevelyan, Coventure, London, 1980
Message in our Time, Pir Vilayat Khan, Harper & Row,
    San Francisco, 1978
Metamorphosis, Robert St John, Metamorphic Association,
    London
Muktananda, Selected Essays, ed. by P. Zweig, Harper & Row,
    London, 1976
Prophet, The, Kahlil Gibran, Heinemann, London, 1976
Reflexology, A. Kaye & D. C. Matchan, Thorsons, England,
    1978
Scientific Healing Affirmations, Paramahansa Yogananda,
    Self-Realization Fellowship, L.A., 1974
Spiritual Midwifery, Ina May Gaskin, Book Pub. Co.,
    Sommertown, TN, 1975
Stalking the Wild Pendulum, I. Bentov, Bantam, New York,
    1979
Tao of Physics, F. Capra, Fontana, London, 1975
Tao of Psychology, J. Shinoda Boles, Wildwood House,
    London, 1980
Tao Te Ching, Lao Tzu, Penguin, London
Tight Corners in Pastoral Counselling, F. Lake, Darton
    Longman & Todd, London, 1981

Notes

Frontpiece: The Song of Self Healing, John Shane, Dec 1978
1. Scientific Healing Affirmations, Paramahansa Yogananda,
    Self-Realization Fellowship
2. The Glory Which is Earth, Evelyn Nolt
3. Ascent of Man, J. Bronowski, B.B.C. Publications
4. New English Bible, John 13
5. Muktananda, Selected Essays, ed. by Paul Zweig,
    Harper & Row
6. The Sanity Book, James Rudolph Murley
7. Wholistic Phenomenology — Emotion and Consciousness,
    Jonathan Daemion
8. Wholistic Phenomenology — Emotion and Consciousness
9. Meditations on the Endocrine Glands, Earth and Man,
    Dr Karl König
10. Meditations on the Endocrine Glands
11. Newsweek, October 24, 1977
12. The Prophet, Kahlil Gibran, Heinemann
13. Metamorphosis, Robert St John, Metamorphic Association
14. The Bible, Ezekiel 37
15. Bodymind, Ken Dytchwold
16. Bioenergetics, Alexander Lowen
17. Metamorphosis, Robert St John
18. The Prophet, Kahlil Gibran
19. The Bhagavad Gita, The Penguin Classics, Penguin Books
20. Four Quartets, T. S. Eliot
21. The Prophet, Kahlil Gibran
22. Tokujiro Nanikoshi
23. Illusions, Richard Bach

Index

Other Books Published by Element Books

TALKING ABOUT ACUPUNCTURE
J. R. WORSLEY
Paper £2.95

TRADITIONAL CHINESE ACUPUNCTURE
Vol 1 Points and Meridians
J. R. WORSLEY
Cased £45.00

THROUGH MUSIC TO THE SELF
PETER MICHAEL HAMEL
Paper £4.50

THE INVISIBLE WAY
RESHAD FEILD
Paper £4.50

*For our Complete Catalogue
please send s.a.e. to:*

**ELEMENT BOOKS LTD
THE OLD BREWERY
TISBURY
SALISBURY WILTSHIRE
TEL: 0747 870 747**